GLOBAL ORGANIZATIONS

The African Union

GLOBAL ORGANIZATIONS

The African Union

The Arab League

The Association of Southeast Asian Nations

The Caribbean Community and Common Market

The European Union

The International Atomic Energy Agency

The Organization of American States

The Organization of Petroleum
Exporting Countries

The United Nations

The United Nations Children's Fund

The World Bank and
the International Monetary Fund

The World Health Organization

The World Trade Organization

GLOBAL ORGANIZATIONS

The African Union

Diedre L. Badejo

Series Editor
Peggy Kahn
University of Michigan–Flint

CHELSEA HOUSE
PUBLISHERS
An imprint of Infobase Publishing

Chelsea House
An imprint of Infobase Publishing
132 West 31st Street
New York NY 10001

Library of Congress Cataloging-in-Publication Data
Badejo, Diedre.
  The African Union / Diedre L. Badejo.
    p. cm. — (Global organizations)
  Includes bibliographical references and index.
  ISBN: 978-0-7910-9543-0 (hardcover)
  1. African Union. 2. Globalization—Africa. 3. National security—Africa. 4. Africa—Politics and government—1960. I. Title. II. Series.

  DT30.5.B33 2007
  341.24'9—dc22   2007046874

Chelsea House books are available at special discounts when purchased in bulk quantities for businesses, associations, institutions, or sales promotions. Please call our Special Sales Department in New York at (212) 967-8800 or (800) 322-8755.

You can find Chelsea House on the World Wide Web at http://www.chelseahouse.com

Series design by Erik Lindstrom
Cover design by Ben Peterson

Printed in the United States of America

Bang KT 10 9 8 7 6 5 4 3 2 1

This book is printed on acid-free paper.

All links and Web addresses were checked and verified to be correct at the time of publication. Because of the dynamic nature of the Web, some addresses and links may have changed since publication and may no longer be valid.

CONTENTS

INTRODUCTION

Trouble in Zimbabwe/ Rhodesia

WHITE SETTLERS BEGAN ARRIVING IN THE 1880S IN THE southern African kingdom called Zimbabwe and inhabited by the Shona people, part of the great wave of European settlement and domination of that time. Colonizers renamed the territory Rhodesia after Cecil Rhodes, who dreamed of uniting the whole world under white British rule and made a fortune in diamond, gold, and copper. Opening the way for British settlers, he and his company, the British South African Company, dominated a vast territory, extracting minerals and using the labor of black Africans whom they pushed off the land and controlled by force. Later, the settlers turned toward farming as their main source of livelihood, seizing most of the good farmland and pushing African farmers into ever smaller areas or off the land entirely.

By the 1960s, the call for independence of African countries was sweeping the continent. Africans, many of whom had fought with the European Allies against Nazism and the Axis powers in World War II, believed that they deserved respect and independence after the war, especially since American and British war leaders had been calling for freedom for all. The European powers, depleted after the war and having to rebuild their bombed-out countries, were finding it more difficult and expensive to hold on to colonies. Britain had decided it would only hand over its African colonies to black majority governments. No Independence Before Black African Rule was its policy.

White Rhodesians were outraged that the British were going to take away their power. Instead of cooperating with the British, in 1965 they unilaterally declared independence (UDI) from Britain on the basis of white-only rule. Their prime minister, Ian Smith, insisted that he was protecting justice, civilization, and Christianity and that he was holding the line against the expansion of Communism across Africa.

Black Rhodesians rebelled, eventually using weapons. A group called ZANU (Zimbabwe African National Union) was led by Robert Mugabe and received some assistance from China. Another group, ZAPU (Patriotic Front-Zimbabwe African People's Union), was supported by the Soviet Union. Together they represented much of the black population. The white government struck back, organizing the white settlers for war, killing black independence leaders, even resorting to biological warfare, spreading anthrax and other poisons. There were thousands of deaths—as many as 30,000 fighters and civilians, mainly black—and vast population migrations.

In 1963, African countries had formed the Organization of African Unity (OAU) to unite the African continent and to help end colonialism and apartheid, or official racial separation, in South Africa. The OAU had a committee to channel

When British colonial rule ended and the struggle for power of Rhodesia began, Robert Mugabe was on the frontlines of the battle between black and white. His organization, the Zimbabwean African National Union, fought against the white minority in order to return the black majority to power in Africa.

money and military aid to liberation movements. Because Britain failed to forcefully oppose the defiant, unilateral declaration of independence (UDI) by the white settlers, the OAU recommended that African countries break their diplomatic relations with Britain. This helped ensure that no other countries would recognize Rhodesia as a legitimate government and that the United Nations would call for economic sanctions. In December 1966, *Time* magazine reported:

The United Nations Security Council last week took a historic step, of sorts. For the first time in its 21 years of existence it resorted to mandatory sanctions to bring down a government. Object of the sanctions was Ian Smith's white supremacist regime in Rhodesia... By a vote of 11 to 0—with four abstentions—the Council declared an international embargo on 90% of Rhodesia's exports, forbade the U.N.'s 122-member nation's to sell oil, arms, motor vehicles or airplanes or provide any form of "financial or other economic aid."[1]

In the late 1970s, the United States and the United Kingdom and various groups of Rhodesians held a conference aimed at creating a peaceful settlement. The Lancaster House agreement they signed put in place a democratic system for Rhodesia, but it contained special protection for the white settlers. They automatically got a number of seats in the Parliament, the representative body, and white-owned land, originally seized from black farmers, was protected as private property. However, the agreement stipulated that land could be transferred from white farmers to blacks on a willing buyer, willing seller basis and raised the expectation that there would be considerable land redistribution.

On April 18, 1980, the country became independent as the Republic of Zimbabwe, with a capital at Harare, and Mugabe's party was in power as the result of an election supervised by international bodies. To keep white Rhodesians from leaving in the new situation of black rule, Mugabe promised that changes would be made gradually and according to law. At first the country was stable and prosperous, but white farmers resisted sale of their land. Britain and the international community did little to lessen this resistance. Yet expectations of a return of the land to its original black farmers had been high, especially among war veterans.

Twenty-five years later Mugabe is still in power but the promise of independence has been tarnished, and Zimbabwe is collapsing economically and politically. Because the small white population continued to own most of the farming land, a legacy of colonialism, Mugabe's government tried to carry out a change in land ownership. But some of these transfers of land involved violence, and many people claim that the land went primarily to Mugabe's friends and allies. The chaos in the countryside led to a decline in food production and a decrease in the export of agricultural goods.

In 2005, the government demolished the homes of about 700,000 city dwellers. Mugabe said that "Operation Drive Out Rubbish" was necessary to "restore sanity" to Zimbabwe's cities, which he said were full of criminals, dirty, and dangerous. Opposition leaders said Mugabe was harassing city dwellers, who generally supported them instead of the ruling party. Human rights supporters said the government had denied basic rights to safety, homes, and health care. In general, say human rights organizations, police in Zimbabwe arbitrarily arrest and beat activists, use unnecessary force to disrupt peaceful demonstrations, and possibly torture those they have arrested. Laws prevent criticism of the government.

With little food, little fuel, little work, and little basic security, people have fled the cities and countryside. Refugees are streaming into neighboring countries, including South Africa. There are many displaced people within the country. The health system has collapsed, and women are expected to live only 34 years, and men 37. The value of money is so low that it takes huge amounts to buy anything. The price of gas, for instance, is 85,000 Zimbabwean dollars per liter and rising.

The OAU has been replaced by a new organization of the continent, the African Union (AU). Now that colonialism and South African apartheid have ended, it intends to emphasize good government, democracy and rule of law, economic growth, and social progress. What will or can the AU do about Zimbabwe? Can it live up to its new promise of enforcing human rights and good government and find a constructive solution that would be an African solution to African problems, one of the main goals of the AU?

Leaders in the AU and the South African Development Community have said that the people of Zimbabwe should be allowed to elect the leaders of their choice in an atmosphere of peace, and they have praised South African President Thabo Mbeki's efforts to help Mugabe and his opposition talk with one another. The African Commission on Human and Peoples' Rights, a special body in the African Union, has condemned Zimbabwe's human rights practices. In 2005, they sent an observer to undertake a fact-finding mission, but he was not allowed into the country. The current Nigerian president, Umaru Musa Yar'Adua, has strongly said that Mugabe's government has failed to respect the rule of law. Others in the AU claim that Mugabe is a hero of African independence, or say that the West should focus on other problems in Africa. In these difficult circumstances, the AU is trying to develop an effective course of action.

Introduction to
the African Union

THE AFRICAN UNION (AU), FOUNDED IN 2002, REPRESENTS the fifty-three nations on the African continent. It is the successor to the Organization of African Unity (OAU), which was founded in 1963 and worked to bring African nations together to gain and strengthen their independence from the European nations that had ruled over them, often by force, for many decades.

While the OAU stood against colonialism, apartheid, and dependence on foreign countries, the AU emphasizes democracy, human rights, and economic development. The key mission of the relatively new AU is to create greater unity and cooperation among the member countries and among the peoples of Africa in order to improve living conditions on the continent. The 53 member nations hope that the organization will make it possible for African countries to be heard in global discussions and negotiations.

Admission to membership in the AU is open to any African state that accepts its founding treaty and expresses the desire to become a member. Membership is refused to governments that come to power through "unconstitutional means," such as military coups, overthrowing of civilian governments, or corrupt elections. Under the OAU, no such provision existed. An article in the AU treaty also provides for the suspension of existing member states that fall to unconstitutional governments.

The main bodies of the AU include an Assembly of the Heads of State and Government of the member states, an Executive Council, a Pan-African Parliament, and a Commission. The AU works with governments of the member states and with other international organizations such as the European Union and the United Nations. Sometimes it has projects with nongovernmental organizations such as Doctors Without Borders and the International Red Cross. AU member states are also members of the United Nations and other international organizations.

AN ORGANIZATION ON THE CONTINENT OF AFRICA

The AU is composed of countries on the continent of Africa, the second largest land mass on Earth with more than 20 percent of the human population, about 770 million people. Africa is spread across all four hemispheres—Eastern, Northern, Western, and Southern—and includes both tropical and subtropical climate zones. The continent is so large that the United States, China, India, and Australia could fit inside of it. Four of the world's longest rivers—the Nile, the Niger, the Zaire, and the Zambesi—traverse Africa.

Human culture on the African continent is both old and richly diverse. Paleoanthropologists such as the Leakey family,

African Union

MOROCCO
TUNISIA
ALGERIA
LIBYA
EGYPT
WESTERN* SAHARA
CAPE VERDE
MAURITANIA
MALI
NIGER
CHAD
ERITREA
SUDAN
DJIBOUTI
SENEGAL
THE GAMBIA
GUINEA-BISSAU
GUINEA
BURKINA FASO
NIGERIA
GHANA
SIERRA LEONE
LIBERIA
CÔTE D'IVOIRE
TOGO BENIN
EQ. GUINEA
CAMEROON
CENTRAL AFRICAN REPUBLIC
ETHIOPIA
SOMALIA
UGANDA
KENYA
CONGO
GABON
RWANDA
DEM. REP. of the CONGO
SÃO TOMÉ AND PRÍNCIPE
Cabinda (ANGOLA)
BURUNDI
TANZANIA
SEYCHELLES
ATLANTIC OCEAN
ANGOLA
ZAMBIA
MALAWI
COMOROS
NAMIBIA
ZIMBABWE
BOTSWANA
MOZAMBIQUE
MADAGASCAR
MAURITIUS
SWAZILAND
SOUTH AFRICA
LESOTHO
INDIAN OCEAN

African Union member

* The government in exile for Western Sahara is an African Union member.

Source: CIA World Factbook 1999

0   800 miles
0   800 km

© Infobase Publishing

Although Morocco is not a member of the AU (it opposes the membership of Western Sahara), it has special status within the AU and benefits from the services available to the other 53 member nations.

Kamoya Kimeu, Donald Johanson, and Owen Lovejoy, among others, have uncovered rich traces of the earliest humans throughout the continent. Africa has been home to many civilizations and cultures, with early-recorded civilization developing around the Nile River and giving rise to dynastic Egypt from about 3100 B.C. to 332 B.C. Other kingdoms and cultures developed along the lower Nile, the Niger River, and on the eastern coast of the continent on the Indian Ocean. Arabic-speaking Muslims entered northern Africa in the seventh century and have been an important influence on the continent, especially in the north and east. Africa has more than 2,000 ethno-linguistic cultures.

The African continent is divided into six ecosystems or vegetation zones that straddle several countries and, as in the case of the Nile River, contribute to Africa's beauty but also to its regional tensions and conflicts. Its ecosystems include the Mediterranean, tropical grassland, hot desert, mountain region, dry grassland, and tropical rain forest. Africa includes five major deserts including the world's largest, the Sahara, and its oldest, the Namib. Only 6 percent of the continent is arable, or usable for growing food crops. Both the age of the continent and the relative inactivity of most of its volcanoes contribute to the lack of fertility in many parts of Africa. Twenty-five percent of the continent is made up of forest and another 25 percent of pasture and long-distance grazing land.

The shifting patterns of Africa's ecosystems, growing populations, political upheavals, and now global warming and climate change have contributed to many centuries of migration throughout and beyond the continent. Such migrations place additional burdens on the neighboring countries, many of which are themselves faced with limited internal resources for their own populations. This is currently the case in Chad and Uganda in eastern Africa. As the population grows and more people move from rural to urban areas, African leaders and nations must deal with increasing challenges from food crises, soil erosion and deforestation, drought, famine, and disease.

THE IMPACT OF COLONIALISM AND APARTHEID IN AFRICA

Africa's modern history is indelibly marked by modern European colonialism. Although colonialism came later to Africa than to other areas such as Latin America, and it was relatively brief, it had a serious, and even devastating, impact. European powers conquered Africa in the late nineteenth and early twentieth centuries. By the 1960s, most African countries were winning their independence, their right to govern themselves.

The European Scramble for Africa at the end of the 1800s is probably the best-known part of this colonial history. Britain, France, and Portugal had economic interests in Africa's resources and had already established outposts on the coasts. Germany, Italy, and Belgium under King Leopold also became involved in the struggle for Africa's riches. These European countries sometimes worked together and sometimes fought each other in Africa for control of territory. On occasion, African rulers and local leaders negotiated and agreed to be ruled from outside. In the cases where the Africans fought back fiercely, they had to battle the Europeans' superior industrial and military technology and even the Africans the colonial rulers recruited from different regions to fight on their side. The Europeans generally defeated any African peoples who resisted.

Europeans carved up Africa to suit their interests, often dividing groups of people with a shared culture, throwing together other groups whose cultures were very different. Some countries, especially France, dismantled the ruling structures that Africans themselves had built, declaring Africans subjects of France but ruling the African colonies according to harsh laws that were not in effect in France. The British tended to use existing rulers, like the emirs in northern Nigeria. Europeans told themselves and Africans that Africans were too backward and primitive to govern themselves.

European colonialism in Africa meant the exploitation of Africa's natural and human resources for the benefit of the colonial governments rather than the African population. For example, European manufacturers processed the oil from African palm trees to make soaps and cooking oils. Although Africans use palm oil for cooking and other domestic purposes, the colonial governments determined how much they could keep for their own use, how much they could sell it for, and to whom they could sell it. During the colonial era, many West African farmers were forced to plant cacao trees, which are a source of cosmetics, soaps, cocoa butter, and chocolate. Most of the cacao was exported, since few Africans eat chocolate or drink cocoa. Colonial demand forced African farmers to use much of their limited arable land for what were known as cash crops, such as cacao, for export to foreign powers. The colonial demand for cash crops and other raw materials left little land for domestic crops and changed the ways that Africans used their farmland. Moreover, African women have always played an important role in farming, providing for their families and communities, and the colonial demands forced changes in the ways they and other members of their communities functioned.

European colonialism also prevented the development of other industries by restricting what people produced and how they traded. For example, African people are known for their beautiful clothing and creative styles as well as their weaving. During the colonial era, they were often required to abandon their own clothing materials and styles and adopt Western dress. They were made to purchase clothing manufactured in foreign countries and to pay for it in colonial currencies. Many people abandoned their way of life to pursue work in the colonial administration or in foreign labor markets that paid them in wages they could use to pay colonial taxes and later to exchange for the newly imported food and clothing.

For centuries African societies had been known for their long-distance trade and regional trading centers. Many kingdoms expanded their trade across regions and reached destinations in southern Europe, Asia, and northeastern Africa. The introduction of colonial domination interrupted these large-scale trade routes and kingdoms. Nonetheless, Africans found many ways to resist this European domination and fight for national independence. After fighting with the Allies in World War II, Africans were inspired to fight to regain their own independence, and they were encouraged by talk of democratic values during the war. African soldiers who fought with British armies had been told that they were fighting against fascist and Nazi regimes, which were undemocratic and wanted to expand beyond their borders to rule other peoples. In the Atlantic Charter issued in 1941, British Prime Minister Winston Churchill and U.S. President Franklin Roosevelt stated that the Allies "respect the right of all peoples to choose the form of government under which they will live; and they will wish to see sovereign rights of self-government restored to those who have been forcibly deprived of them."[2] World War II also weakened the major colonial powers—Britain, France, and Germany—and the United States and the Soviet Union emerged as superpowers.

As Africans won their independence in the 1960s and 1970s, they were faced with many challenges. The way Africans had governed themselves was distorted by colonial rule, and their new states were artificial creations of the Europeans. They had few resources to support their states, and few Africans had received training in the ways of modern statecraft, business, and economics. In addition, their economies had been oriented toward trade with Europe, often depending upon a few resources or crops. In Africa the desire for political independence was always tied to the desire for economic independence and development. The people of Africa wanted to be able to shape their own economies and create more wealth for the development of their societies.

South Africa did not remain a formal colony for long. In 1910, it became an independent republic, yet until 1994 it remained under the control of white European settlers. The white settlers, descendants of both the original Dutch and British settlers, were a small minority of the population of the territory. The Dutch, called Afrikaners, were the majority of the whites. In 1948, the South African government, controlled by an Afrikaner political party, created a system of

African Independence

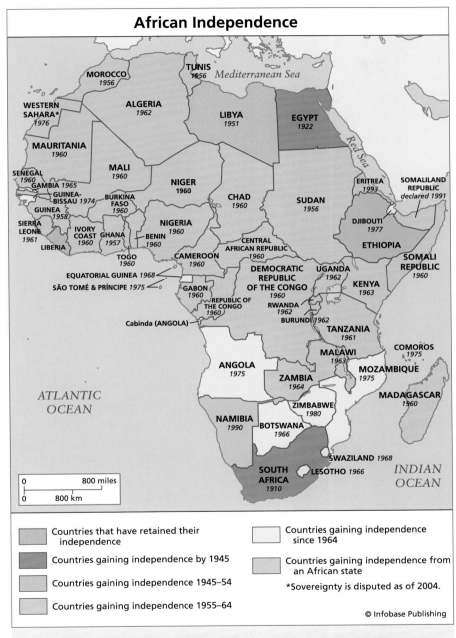

MOROCCO
1956

TUNIS
1956   *Mediterranean Sea*

WESTERN
SAHARA*
1976

ALGERIA
1962

LIBYA
1951

EGYPT
1922

MAURITANIA
1960

MALI
1960

NIGER
1960

CHAD
1960

SUDAN
1956

ERITREA
1993

SOMALILAND
REPUBLIC
declared 1991

Red Sea

SENEGAL
1960
GAMBIA 1965
GUINEA-
BISSAU 1974
GUINEA
1958

BURKINA
FASO
1960

DJIBOUTI
1977

ETHIOPIA

SOMALI
REPUBLIC
1960

SIERRA
LEONE
1961
LIBERIA

IVORY
COAST GHANA
1960   1957

BENIN
1960

NIGERIA
1960

CENTRAL
AFRICAN REPUBLIC
1960

TOGO
1960

CAMEROON
1960

DEMOCRATIC
REPUBLIC
OF THE CONGO
1960

UGANDA
1962

KENYA
1963

EQUATORIAL GUINEA 1968

SÃO TOMÉ & PRÍNCIPE 1975

GABON
1960

REPUBLIC OF
THE CONGO
1960

RWANDA
1962

Cabinda (ANGOLA)

BURUNDI 1962

TANZANIA
1961

COMOROS
1975

MALAWI
1963

MOZAMBIQUE
1975

ANGOLA
1975

ZAMBIA
1964

MADAGASCAR
1960

ATLANTIC
OCEAN

ZIMBABWE
1980

NAMIBIA
1990

BOTSWANA
1966

SWAZILAND 1968

SOUTH
AFRICA
1910

LESOTHO 1966

INDIAN
OCEAN

0   800 miles

0   800 km

Countries that have retained their
independence

Countries gaining independence
since 1964

Countries gaining independence by 1945

Countries gaining independence from
an African state

Countries gaining independence 1945–54

*Sovereignty is disputed as of 2004.

Countries gaining independence 1955–64

© Infobase Publishing

In the late nineteenth century, European imperial powers engaged in a major territorial scramble, called the Scramble for Africa. European rule over African nations continued until the end of World War II, when all colonial states gradually obtained formal independence.

Apartheid became a system of racial divide in South Africa, with the government assigning each citizen into one of three categories: white, black, or colored (of mixed descent). This system blocked black Africans from opportunities to improve their social and economic status, forcing them to endure a lower standard of living. For example, shops like this would often advertise cheaper, second-grade meat for black Africans and servants.

brutal legal segregation in every sphere of life. The system of apartheid stripped the majority indigenous African population of its human rights and used violence to enforce segregation, transfer of land, and to suppress opposition. Only whites could vote and they reserved the best jobs and places to live for themselves. Black Africans had no rights and were not regarded as citizens of South Africa. They were forcibly moved out of reserved white areas and dumped into dusty, infertile lands or packed into poor townships near cities, used as cheap labor on farms and in mines, often separated from their families and required to have written permission, or passes, to travel to see them. Partly on the backs of black labor, South Africa built a diversified, relatively industrial economy, the largest in Africa. Apartheid only ended in 1994, as the white Afrikaners and the anti-apartheid forces led by Nelson Mandela of the African National Congress (ANC) negotiated a peaceful transition to a democracy where race could not be used to determine rights.

AFRICAN POLITICS AND ECONOMIES TODAY

Among the 53 member nations of Africa today, the political systems range from democracy to authoritarian rule to plain misgovernment, and sometimes a mixture of all three. In many countries, the idealism that led to independence gave way to authoritarianism, bitter civil conflict, and widespread violations of human rights. Many countries came to be ruled by one party that refused to allow for an opposition and democratic competition. There were also many civil wars, wars within the countries. In some instances there were clashes between ethnic groups that had been defined and set against each other by the colonial powers or that had become rivals after independence. Other civil wars were set in motion by the Cold War, in which African countries became pawns of the superpowers, the United States and the Soviet Union.

Since 1990, there has been a widespread but fragile push toward democracy. The most remarkable transition has been in South Africa, but many other countries have tentatively moved in the direction of democracy: free elections, free speech, basic human rights. The Gambia, Senegal, Botswana, and Mauritius have long been democratic, but since 1990 more than 20 additional countries in Africa have had credible elections and ruling parties have left office as a result of defeat at the polls. Other countries, however, have maintained or moved back toward authoritarian rule—Zimbabwe, for example. And in some countries where democracy has been instituted, social and economic progress has been challenging.

African countries stand lowest in the world in the United Nations' ranking of countries by their populations' quality of life. The average resources per person in sub-Saharan Africa is equal to about $840 a year, life expectancy on average is 47 years, and overall enrollment in school is about 95 percent

ARTICLE 3 OF THE CONSTITUTIVE ACT OF THE AFRICAN UNION

Article 3 of the Constitutive Act, the founding document of the AU, states that the purposes of the African Union are to:

a) achieve great unity and solidarity between the African countries and peoples of Africa;

b) defend the sovereignty, territorial integrity, and independence of its Member States;

c) accelerate the political and socio-economic integration of the continent;

d) promote and defend African common positions on issues of interest to the continent and its peoples;

e) encourage international cooperation, taking due account of the Charter of the United Nations and the Universal Declaration of Human Rights;

f) promote peace, security, and stability on the continent;

g) promote democratic principles and institutions, popular participation, and good governance;

h) promote and protect human and peoples' rights in accordance with the African Charter on Human and Peoples' Rights and other relevant human rights instruments;

in primary school but only 31 percent in secondary school, according to the World Bank.[3] Many Africans have no food security, but go hungry or are malnourished. Despite Africa's multitude of great rivers and lakes, much of the population lacks clean drinking water, due partly to drought and problems of transporting water to those who need it. Some foreign assistance to Africa has had good effects, but many grants and loans have been used with little effect. African countries have

i)   establish the necessary conditions which enable the continent to play its rightful role in the global economy and in international negotiations;

j)   promote sustainable development at the economic, social, and cultural levels as well as the integration of African economies;

k)   promote cooperation in all fields of human activity to raise the living standards of African peoples;

l)   coordinate and harmonize the policies between the existing and future Regional Economic Communities for the gradual attainment of the objectives of the Union;

m)   advance the development of the continent by promoting research in all fields, in particular in science and technology; and

n)   work with relevant international partners in the eradication of preventable diseases and the promotion of good health on the continent[*]

[*] African Union, "The Constitutive Act."
Available online at http://www.africa-union.org.

large debts to the richer countries that have lent it money, often for failed development projects and arms. Africa lacks strong transportation networks, such as railroads, paved roadways, and modern ports, as a result of the failure of colonial rule. Many African economies have been growing but are still far below those in other areas of the world.

Against this background, the Organization of African Unity, and later the African Union, developed plans to recapture political control of the continent and focus on good governance and economic development. As the successor to the OAU, the AU is acting to improve governments—increasing expertise, reducing corruption, and strengthening democratic ideas and practices—and to regain control over the African economies, resources, and trade. To make better use of its resources, African leaders are intensifying their planning to focus the education of their young people on the needs of the African regions and governments. It is not surprising that the AU has made economic development—diversified, growing economies based upon better trained and educated workers—a high priority.

Beginnings of
the African Union

FOUNDED BY 32 LEADERS OF INDEPENDENT AFRICAN STATES on May 25, 1963, the mandate of the OAU was to promote the unity of the new African states, to eliminate all forms of colonialism in Africa, to encourage cooperation across the continent, and to defend the sovereignty and territory of each individual African state. Its purpose was to help complete the decolonization of the continent, but its formation was dependent upon the beginning success of African independence. Its founders were many of the political giants on the continent, including Dr. Kwame Nkrumah of Ghana, Léopold Sédar Senghor of Senegal, and Haile Selassie of Ethiopia.

In the late 1940s and early 1950s, new political parties in African countries demanded political freedom and an end to colonial rule. The intensifying of these demands took

Kwame Nkrumah, one of Africa's most famous leaders, became the prime minister of Africa's first country to gain independence from its colonizers. His work to free Ghana from British rule set the stage for other African countries to fight for their right to become independent countries. He was also one of the founding members of the OAU.

European colonial powers by surprise. The Italians and the British, followed by the French and the reluctant Belgians, eventually responded to the calls for independence. Libya gained independence from Italy in 1951. Egypt had received formal independence in 1922, but British troops remained there until 1954. The British also ruled Ghana (formerly called the Gold Coast), which in 1957 was the first country south of the Sahara to become independent. Kwame Nkrumah, who led the independence movement there and began to speak about cooperation among independent African countries, became Ghana's first president. 1960 was the big year for African independence: 14 African countries gained their independence. By 1963, that number had grown to 35.

Some blacks, including W.E.B. Dubois (1868–1963), a famous African American thinker, had begun already in the 1930s to write about Pan-Africanism, an idea that the continent of Africa should be considered an independent homeland for blacks throughout the world, including the United States. Pan-Africanism was believed to be a way to end colonial rule and the arbitrary division of Africa by the colonial powers. African post-colonial leaders such as Ghana's Nkrumah continued to think along these lines. To strengthen the continent of Africa and to make it less vulnerable to outside influence, Nkrumah strongly believed that the continent should be united. He had been the organizing secretary of the Fifth Pan-African Congress held in Manchester, England, in 1945, and while in London he worked with student groups that were ultimately interested in a United States of Africa. In 1958 Nkrumah organized the first Conference of Independent African States and an All-African People's Conference.

When Nkrumah introduced the concept of African unity to the continent, newly independent African states divided into two groups. Some countries and their leaders, including Nkrumah, Sekou Toure of Guinea, and Modibo Keita of Mali preferred immediate and complete unity, even with a unified

(continues on page 30)

KWAME NKRUMAH AND PAN-AFRICANISM

When he wrote his book, *I Speak of Freedom*, in 1961, Kwame
Nkrumah was president of a new country in West Africa, Ghana,
which had finally won its independence from British control in
1957. He wrote:

> For centuries, Europeans dominated the African continent.
> The white man arrogated to himself the right to rule and
> be obeyed by the non-white.... Europeans robbed the con-
> tinent of vast riches and inflicted unimaginable suffering on
> the African people.... All this makes a sad story, but now
> we must be prepared to bury the past with its unpleasant
> memories and look to the future.... It is clear that we must
> find an African solution to our problems and that this can
> only be found in African unity. Divided we are weak; united,
> Africa could become one of the greatest forces for good in
> the world. Never before have a people had within their grasp
> so great an opportunity for developing a continent endowed
> with so much wealth. Individually, the independent states of
> Africa, some potentially rich, others poor, can do little for
> their people. Together, by mutual help, they can achieve much.
> But the economic development of the continent must be
> planned and pursued as a whole.... Only a strong political
> union can bring about full and effective development of our
> natural resources for the benefit of the people.[*]

Nkrumah was a Pan-Africanist. He had been inspired by ear-
lier thinkers who believed that Africans and African descendants
abroad were equally African and one people and that through unity
Africa could become prosperous and dynamic. At the Pan-African
Congress in Manchester, people began to think that the Africans

on the continent of Africa should take the lead to demand their freedom and work to unify Africa.

In Ghana, then called the Gold Coast, Nkrumah helped organize workers, farmers, and young people, men and women, into a political group, the Convention People's Party (CCP), to demand independence. The British arrested Nkrumah after he led protests, but finally they decided to leave and helped to organize an election in the country. Even though he was in prison, Nkrumah and his party won by a landslide. In March 1957, Ghana became the first country in Africa to win its independence, and Nkrumah was hailed as "the victorious one." The 1960 Ghana Constitution included plans for an eventual incorporation of Ghana into an African union. Nkrumah was one of the founders of the Organization of African Unity in 1963.

Once in power, Nkrumah lost some support. He suspected foreign intervention in his government and plans for Ghana. He made strikes illegal, and he introduced a law that made it possible to arrest people without going through the regular courts. He was interested in building industry to reduce Ghana's dependence on foreign trade, but in doing this he hurt many cocoa farmers, whose business was one of Ghana's most lucrative. Nkrumah worked with Ghanaian and international unions, was supported by the Soviet Union, and was interested in the civil rights movement for equality in the United States. Many believe that, in part because of these activities, his government was overthrown in 1966 in a coup by soldiers who seemed to have ties to the U.S. Central Intelligence Agency.

In 1999, people in Africa who listened to the British Broadcasting Corporation (BBC) voted Nkrumah "Man of the Millennium."

* Kwame Nkrumah, "I Speak of Freedom," 1961, in *Modern History Sourcebook*. Available online at *http://www.fordham.edu/halsall/mod/1961nkrumah.html*.

(continued from page 27)

African military. Later on, Egypt, the transitional government of Algeria, and Morocco joined the Ghana-Guinea-Mali Union to form the Casablanca Group.

The other group, called the Monrovia Group, made up of 24 countries including Nigeria, Liberia, Senegal, Ivory Coast, Cameroon, and Togo, believed in a more gradual approach to African unity, combining economies across borders as a first step. Many believed that the rift between the two groups would become permanent and that the hopes for African unity would be dashed.

Yet, in May 1963, these two opposing groups were able to form the OAU. Many have speculated about how agreement grew despite such a sharp division in approach. It appears that all the independent states that came together in Addis Ababa to establish the OAU did so partly because of Emperor Haile Selassie of Ethiopia, who urged unity. He had his reasons. In 1935, Italy was looking for a piece of empire and invaded Ethiopia. Although both Italy and Ethiopia were members of the League of Nations, which was supposed to keep the peace and act against aggression, the league was unable to control Italy or protect Ethiopia. In 1963, Haile Selassie may have thought that an alignment of African countries would protect them from invasion by countries outside the continent. In addition, Ethiopia had recently taken over part of Somalia as well as Eritrea. Inside the OAU, with its principle of nonintervention in each other's affairs, Ethiopia probably felt that these annexations would not be challenged and that their territory was secure. Ethiopia had never been colonized and had no ties to either Britain, which had been dominant in East Africa, or France, which had dominated West Africa, so other African countries might have seen Selassie as a neutral party.

Thus, the OAU was officially established in May 1963 in Addis Ababa, the Ethiopian capital. It was heralded as an organization that would continue to fight colonialism

In May 1963, the OAU held their first conference in Addis Ababa, Ethiopia. Thirty African nations gathered to make a collective effort toward economic development and the end of colonialism in Africa.

and represent African interests on a global scale. Kwamina Panford remembers:

My own first personal encounter with the OAU occurred in Ghana in 1965. I can still vividly recall television scenes from the Second Ordinary Summit of African Heads of State/Government hosted by President Kwame Nkrumah. Like most youth in Ghana or elsewhere in Africa, I also had the expectation that both political independence and the OAU would change Africa's role in the global community. We expected that the OAU—in Nkrumah's words—"would not only ensure the total liberation of Africa but also at the speed of a jet-propelled plane assist the continent in catching up with the developed world in terms of economic development. [4]

The OAU was troubled by two main problems throughout its history. The first was that the Cold War tended to divide African countries, and this division showed up within the organization. The Cold War was the intense rivalry that emerged after World War II between the United States and its allies and the Soviet Union and its allies. The two superpowers competed in political and economic ideas, raced to accumulate more conventional and nuclear weapons, and fought over territory in Africa and Asia, often through local armies. There are some reports that the French used to brief leaders on their way to summits, meetings of the heads of states, urging policies that the West thought were in its interest. The CIA was involved in some of the military coups and the murder of the Congolese prime minister Patrice Lumumba. Pro-U.S. military dictators were supported in Somalia and Kenya. The Soviet Union also had its puppet governments in Ethiopia and elsewhere.

The OAU became divided over which side to support in the Angolan civil war. In this conflict, rival groups fought for control of Angola, which had won independence from Portugal in 1974. One group, the Popular Movement for the Liberation of Angola (Portuguese: Movimento Popular de Libertação de Angola, or MPLA), was backed by Cuba and the Soviet Union. The National Front for the Liberation of Angola (Portuguese: Frente Nacional de Libertação de Angola, or FNLA) was supported by the United States and China. The National Union for the Total Independence of Angola (Portuguese: União Nacional para a Independência Total de Angola, or UNITA) was supported by the United States, U.S. allies, and apartheid South Africa. In December 1975, half the OAU chose one side and half chose the other. This split continued through conflicts in the Democratic Republic of the Congo, during Somalia's invasion of Ethiopia in 1978, and during a conflict between Uganda and Tanzania in 1978 and 1979.

A second problem was related to the instability of African states and the weak norms of democracy. The OAU had been forced into a compromise at its founding: It would not interfere in the internal affairs of other member states. This was partly a condition that grew out of the colonial legacy and partly the way rulers tried to safeguard their own countries against outside interference. The OAU also felt bound by the UN Declaration on the Granting of Independence to Colonial Peoples and Countries, which stated: "All States shall observe faithfully and strictly the provisions of the Charter of the United Nations, the Universal Declaration of Human Rights, and the present Declaration on the basis of equality, non-interference in the internal affairs of all States, and respect for the sovereign rights of all peoples and their territorial integrity."[5] The OAU had no authority to punish illegal governments or intervene in civil strife and genocide. The inability of the OAU to act against authoritarian rulers, those who ruled without the participation of their populations and violated the rule of law, within its own organization earned it the name "the dictator's club."

Despite these splits and weaknesses, the OAU was able to mediate some border disputes in Africa. It helped resolve conflicts between Algeria and Morocco in 1964 and 1965. Conflicts over borders between Somalia and both Ethiopia and Kenya were resolved with the OAU's help. The organization formed an African Liberation Committee in 1963 to channel financial support to movements trying to defeat Portuguese colonial rule in Guinea Bissau, Angola, and Mozambique. These movements were victorious in 1974. It supported movements against white minority rule in South Africa, Rhodesia (now Zimbabwe), and Namibia. It helped bar apartheid South Africa from the UN General Assembly and other UN agencies.

Yet, 30 years after its founding and with the Cold War over, Africa continued to be marginalized in world politics and struggled to find its place in the global economy. Few of Africa's problems had been successfully addressed. The superpowers seemed to be withdrawing from the region, which created a greater possibility of unity on the continent but also meant they were distancing themselves from responsibility for Africa. Several important African leaders believed it was necessary to revive the continent and that African countries needed to practice good government and free-market economics to attract foreign investment.

FROM OAU TO AU

The OAU had actually begun to work on furthering the purposes of good government, economic development, and social progress that would become the objectives of the AU. It took action to support self-reliance, cooperation, coordination, and development among economies. It made efforts to support human rights, root out corruption, insist upon constitutional governments, encourage popular participation in politics, and link and support economies.

It also began to think about how to integrate African nations into a more powerful, cohesive intracontinental organization. Then in Sirte, Libya, in July 1999, the Assembly of Heads of State and Government of the Organization of African Unity came together for an "extraordinary session," only the fourth such session in the OAU's history. African leaders adopted the Sirte Declaration. In it, the heads of government said they wanted to establish a new African union and accelerate the building of new institutions with the African Economic Community as part of a new African union.

This meeting was hosted enthusiastically by the Libyan head of state since 1969, Muammar Qaddafi, who had become a strong supporter of the idea of African unity. Qaddafi is a long-surviving and extremely controversial post-colonial leader in Africa. His political support for the Arab bloc of countries in Africa during the early years of the OAU seemed to contribute to a split along Muslim and non-Muslim lines. Qaddafi is now an ardent supporter of the AU. With surprising speed, within one year of the Sirte Declaration, the founding document of the African Union, called the Constitutive Act, was drafted and circulated to all the member governments. In 2000, in Lome, the capital of Togo, heads of government approved the African Union Constitutive Act, which established and defined the purpose of the new AU and created new organs and bodies, including a council of government ministers, a parliament, and a court.

The Constitutive Act defines the objectives and purposes of the new AU: economic development that can be sustained over time, good governance, social justice, gender equality, youth development, and good health. The African Union Constitutive Act reaffirms the principles of domestic sovereignty and nonintervention. It states that all members recognize the sovereignty of member countries, their right to have their borders respected, and their independence. However, it allows intervention by the AU as a body concerned with peace, security, and stability in the region, in the event of internal conflict in a country. Article 4 of the founding Act provides for "the right of the Union to intervene in a Member State [following] a decision of the Assembly in respect of grave circumstances, namely: war crimes, genocide, and crimes against humanity."[6] The other possibilities for intervention require a decision of the Union's heads of governments. The founding act of the African Union makes it likely that the Union can provide leadership in certain conflicts and in situations where human rights are being violated.

There are also provisions for how the Union will work and what organs will move its goals forward. The main bodies include the Assembly of the Heads of State and Government; an executive council; a Pan-African Parliament; a court of justice;

a commission; a permanent representatives' committee; special technical committees; an economic, social and cultural council; and several special banks.

In 2002, the heads of states of the AU convened in Durban, South Africa, for back-to-back meetings. At first they met as the OAU. United Nations Secretary-General Kofi Annan, himself born and raised in Ghana, spoke to the OAU on the eve of its reorganization as the AU. He warned that it would not be easy to achieve the AU goals of economic progress and good governance. He promoted economic integration, or combining the African economies, as the way forward for the continent but conceded that the poor infrastructure, burden of debt, and political conflicts on the continent presented huge challenges to social and economic progress. "To build a successful union in such conditions will require great stamina and iron political will," he said. But he also maintained that such work on the continent was essential if Africa wanted other countries to forgive some of their debt or for wealthier countries to give aid. "They will respect us even more when they actually see us resolve the conflicts that disfigure our continent. And I do mean resolve them. Managing them is not enough."[7]

On Tuesday, July 9, 2002, the AU was re-launched under new rules and with new objectives. Thabo Mbeki of South Africa was its first chair. Mbeki, who succeeded Nelson Mandela as president of South Africa, has been a powerful figure in African politics. He believes that African political conflicts should be resolved primarily by Africans rather than outsiders and that the AU and its economic partnerships are important to the processes that will make Africa more self-reliant. The first decision of the new AU was to uphold a controversial decision of the OAU not to recognize Madagascar's Marc Ravalomanana as the country's new president, saying he had taken power unconstitutionally. The AU insisted that Madagascar would have to hold a new, fair presidential election before the country could join it.

As international influences withdrew from Africa's political arena, African leaders realized the OAU must also evolve with the changing needs of the entire continent. Working together, these leaders revised the goals and methods of the OAU and transitioned this organization into the African Union. Here, UN Secretary-General Kofi Annan *(left)* greets Zambian President Levy Mwanawasa *(rear)*, South African President Thabo Mbeki, and OAU Secretary-General Amar Essy *(right)* as they arrive for the 38th OAU Summit in Durban, South Africa.

Many African political leaders have thought of the new AU as similar to the European Union (EU), which now has 27 member states that have delegated significant law-making powers to the EU institutions. These bodies are empowered to regulate what is now a Europe-wide economy in many respects, with no tariffs or taxes on imports between European countries, with a common policy toward agricultural goods and prices, a single currency (the euro), EU-wide regulations for product safety and quality, and other common economic rules. The EU is comprised of relatively wealthy countries, all of which, if they are to belong, must be democracies respecting human rights.

The AU has moved the work of the OAU forward and recognizes the great challenges ahead for Africa in the twenty-first century. Its organizational structure; mechanisms for conflict resolution; and attention to economic, political, social, and cultural justice show that the AU upholds a broad vision of progress for the African continent.

How the AU Works

THE 53 AFRICAN NATIONS IN THE AU OPERATE THE ORGANI-
zation through a structure established in the Constitutive Act
adopted in July 2000. The responsibilities, powers, and rules
of the various parts of the AU are specified in that act, though
debates about the interpretation of certain parts of the act continue. The AU carries out its business through many organs,
agencies, and nongovernmental organizations. The institutions
are supported by an AU budget of about $43 million dollars.

There are two major changes in how the organization works
now as the AU as compared with the OAU. There is more scope
for Union intervention, and several new bodies have been
formed to ensure a greater degree of awareness and enforcement of the decisions of the main bodies of the organization,

Structure of the African Union

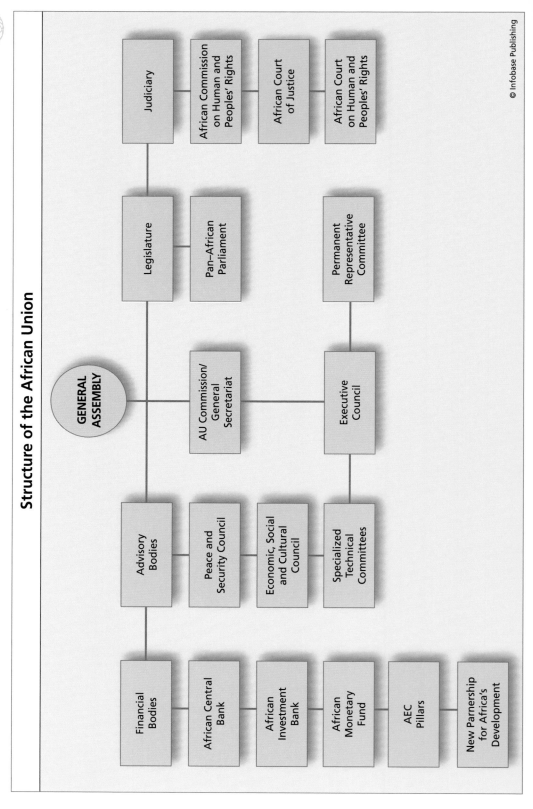

- **GENERAL ASSEMBLY**
  - **Financial Bodies**
    - African Central Bank
    - African Investment Bank
    - African Monetary Fund
    - AEC Pillars
    - New Parnership for Africa's Development
  - **Advisory Bodies**
    - Peace and Security Council
    - Economic, Social and Cultural Council
    - Specialized Technical Committees
  - **AU Commission/ General Secretariat**
    - Executive Council
      - Permanent Representative Committee
  - **Legislature**
    - Pan–African Parliament
  - **Judiciary**
    - African Commission on Human and Peoples' Rights
    - African Court of Justice
    - African Court on Human and Peoples' Rights

the General Assembly of Heads of State and Government and the Executive Council of Ministers.

THE ASSEMBLY, EXECUTIVE COUNCIL OF MINISTERS, AND THE COMMISSION

The General Assembly is the supreme operating unit or organ of the AU. It consists of the African heads of state and government or their representatives meeting together to debate and pass resolutions. Most of these resolutions originate in other agencies and committees and come to the assembly from the Executive Council of Ministers. The council, which determines the common policies of the AU, has a system of democratic voting, with one vote granted to each member state.

The Executive Council is made up of the ministers of foreign affairs from the member countries. Ministers of foreign affairs, similar to the secretary of state in the United States, are top government officials responsible for conducting relationships with other countries and international organizations. These ministers are appointed by their countries and carry out the directions of their governments. The Executive Council of Foreign Ministers meets at least twice a year, sometimes more often. The ministers must act on items sent to them by the General Assembly, and work to carry out those decisions. They aim for consensus or agreement and, if that fails, they decide based on a majority vote. The decisions of the council must go to the General Assembly for discussion and a final vote, meaning the resolutions are passed twice, once by the council and once by the assembly. Because there is a great deal of work to do and complex information to keep up with and because foreign ministers do many things in addition to participating in the AU, a Permanent Representatives' Committee (PRC) prepares the agenda and information for the council and works to carry out its decisions.

The African Union Commission is sometimes called the administrative branch of the AU. There are 10 commissioners, each with responsibility for a particular topic or topics of policy—peace and security; politics and government; energy;

social affairs; science and technology; agriculture; industry and trade; economy; women, gender, and development; budgeting; human resources; and law. The assembly appoints the chair of the commission. The commission is responsible for carrying out the AU's decisions and also coordinates the AU as a whole.

HOW DECISIONS ARE MADE: THE IMPORTANCE OF SUMMITS

The African Union often works through summits, intense meetings of high-level institutions culminating in a meeting of the heads of state and government. First the Permanent Representatives' Committee meets, then the Executive Council meets, and finally the Assembly of Heads of State and Government meets. Like most international and intergovernmental organizations, many lower-level representatives prepare the groundwork for the negotiators and decision-makers. These institutions work together to ensure that perspectives and issues are communicated at each level of authority and that the Assembly of Heads of States and Government receive the most-well-prepared documents possible so that it can make the best decisions.

So, for example, the Eighth African Union Summit occurred between January 22 and January 30, 2007. The PRC met from January 22–23, the Executive Council met from January 25–26, and the AU Assembly, from January 29–30. This round of meetings considered two main, important themes for the African continent: climate change in Africa and science and technology.

While Africa has contributed less to global warming than other continents, it is probably the most vulnerable to the effects of climate change. The Intergovernmental Panel on Climate Change warns that climate change puts African water resources, food supplies, and natural resources at risk. It also may increase water- and insect-borne diseases, make

Despite contributing less to global warming than other, more-developed countries, Africa seems to be feeling the effects of climate change more heavily than other continents. Deserts are growing, droughts are lasting longer, and rising seawater is taking over coastal areas like this one in Alexandria, Egypt.

coastal areas more vulnerable to rises in sea level and "extreme events," and spread deserts over greater areas. After hearing some speeches about these problems from a UN body, the Assembly of Heads of State and Government endorsed several decisions and declarations from the Executive Council of Ministers and adopted many decisions oriented toward helping African countries manage the impact of climate change. The leaders noted the new reports being issued on climate change and development in Africa, expressed grave concern about the vulnerability of Africa's economies and the limited science and technology they had available to help manage change. They endorsed an action plan, urged member states and all partner organizations to integrate climate-change considerations into all their programs for development, and requested that the commission and other AU bodies continue to report on progress. The assembly was unable to agree on developing an Africa-wide science fund or an Africa-wide strategy on safety related to biological materials.[8]

One of the key debates among leaders at the Ninth African Union Summit in July 2007 was the idea of a Pan-African government, a government that would make policies for all African countries. Many leaders raised their voices calling for stronger powers of governing and building a continental government for Africa. "The slow approach toward the formation of the African Union government is a fallacious argument intended to slow down the process," Senegalese President Abdoulaye Wade said at the Ninth Summit of the African heads of state in Accra, Ghana. "Those who support this gradual or step-by-step approach are only delaying the political integration process of the continent."[9] Muammar Qaddafi of Libya also argued that Africa needs "one sole African government, one sole African army to defend Africa with a force of two million soldiers. One currency, one passport. . . . Africa must forbid all war, civil, tribal, or over borders. The youth of Africa is drowning in the Mediterranean to cross the channel to Europe, leaving behind it the paradise which is Africa. No more emigration, no more emigration."[10] The head of the African Union Commission said that Africans need "to take the bull by the horns" and move forward toward a new, united Africa.[11]

Others urged a cautious and careful pace of integration. The president of Uganda, Yoweri Museveni, said that he was against an African continental government because it would create tension, not cohesion, and would force countries to give up their national identity. He preferred strengthening bonds between countries within regions of Africa that may share cultural and economic ties. At the same time, Africa could address certain functions at the continental level:

environment, trade, and defense. Several leaders were also concerned that talking so much about future governing structures in Africa was distracting the attention of leaders from crises in Zimbabwe, Somalia, and Darfur. The African heads of state decided to work toward a government for the entire African continent but set no timetable.[12]

THE PAN-AFRICAN PARLIAMENT AND OTHER BODIES

In 2004, the AU introduced a new, but important organ called the Pan-African Parliament. This body is a critical part of the plan to connect the AU more closely to the peoples of Africa. Right now, the Parliament only consults and advises, but the AU hopes that this organ will eventually become a full partner in decision making with the other major bodies. Currently the members are elected or appointed by the legislatures of their countries, but the AU plans for it to become a body elected directly by citizens of the member countries on a one-person, one-vote basis. There are now 202 members of the Parliament from 41 of the 53 member states; each country has five sitting members. Initially the Parliament was located in Addis Ababa, Ethiopia, but it later moved to Midrand, South Africa.

The Parliament has 10 permanent committees that focus on different themes: rural economies, the environment, and resources; money and finance; trade, customs, and immigration; cooperation and conflict; transportation, industry, energy, and science; health, labor, and social affairs; education, culture, and tourism; gender, family, and youth; justice and human rights; and rules, privileges, and discipline within the Parliament itself.

Like the OAU before it, the AU has its own Peace and Security Council to prevent, manage, and resolve conflicts. The powers of the Peace and Security Council exercised in conjunction with the commission are to authorize peacekeeping missions on the continent; recommend intervention

Because African countries are prone to shifting governments and political upheaval, preventing, managing, and resolving conflict became an important aspect of the AU. Much like the peacekeepers, soldiers from member countries are gathered together to create the AU peacekeeping forces to help maintain order in places like Somalia and Darfur.

in a member state if the circumstances are grave, involving war crimes, genocide, and crimes against humanity; initiate sanctions if there is an unconstitutional change in government, such as a military coup; follow up progress toward good democratic practices and respect for human rights; and support humanitarian actions during armed conflict or natural disasters. African ministers of foreign affairs will elect to the council 15 countries, three from each of Africa's five geographic regions (Western Africa, Central Africa, Eastern Africa, Northern Africa, and Southern Africa). Not only must the members be elected, but the countries serving on this important peacekeeping body will have to meet certain other tests: They must have contributed to recent peacekeeping efforts; made financial contributions to the AU and the Peace Fund; and shown their respect for constitutional government, rule of law, and human rights. The council, collaborating with the UN and other relevant groups, is developing an early warning system, a sort of situation room that will monitor what is happening in the member states and look for warning signs of conflict. Whether this body can be effective remains to be seen, but many people and leaders hope that it will play a constructive role. It has recommended action in Sudan, Liberia, Sierra Leone, and other trouble spots.

The African Court on Human and Peoples' Rights has a potential to make the AU relevant to the way African states treat their populations. The court will only hear cases from the 15 states that have signed the document setting it up, and it should help make up for some of the shortcomings of the African Commission on Human and Peoples' Rights. Under the OAU, it was not only always underfunded, but also unknown to most Africans and unable to take action on human rights abuses. The findings of the new human rights court will be binding and final. Currently, only governments and certain intergovernmental organizations can bring cases to the court, even though the first draft of its powers allowed individuals working with nongovernmental organizations, such as human rights groups, to bring cases.

The Economic, Social and Cultural Council (ECOSOCC) is an advisory body that provides an opportunity for organizations to which ordinary people in Africa might belong—such as youth organizations, women's groups, environmental organizations, health organizations—to contribute to discussions and actions in the AU. Of the 150 groups that have a place in this council, two must come from each member state; 24 come from groups that work in more than one country; and 20 groups must represent the African diaspora—Africans living outside the continent because of the slave trade and forced labor, their fear of remaining in Africa due to persecution or political violence, or voluntary migration. Half the members of the council must be women and half must be youth between the ages of 18 and 35. Like the parliament, this council tries to connect ordinary people and everyday lives to the AU decision-making structure.

TECHNICAL COMMITTEES AND FINANCIAL INSTITUTIONS

Other AU bodies include specialized technical committees and the financial institutions such as the African Central Bank and the African Monetary Fund. The AU Constitutive Act defines how each of these units will function and what duties each will be assigned. The technical committees include the Committee on Rural Economy and Agricultural Matters; the Committee on Monetary and Financial Affairs; the Committee on Trade, Customs and Immigration Matters; the Committee on Industry, Science and Technology, Energy, Natural Resources and Environment; the Committee on Transport, Communications and Tourism; the Committee on Health, Labor and Social Affairs; and the Committee on Education, Culture and Human Resources. The Natural Resources Committee, for example, might work on issues of water, a resource that is unevenly distributed throughout the continent and contributes to the patterns of drought and refugee problems in various regions. The committees are charged with exploring these problems, seeking approaches that may involve compromises, and forming resolutions.

The African Central Bank is intended to strengthen the economies and trade of the member states. Over time, it may create a single African currency that would facilitate trade and travel across borders. Among its many responsibilities and objectives will be establishing rules and processes for regulating interest and exchange rates and public and private investments, as well as regulating Africa's banking industry.

Politics
and Security:
The Trouble
with Borders

ONE OF THE MOST TROUBLING EFFECTS OF COLONIALISM resulted from the arbitrary way in which the colonial powers divided Africa amongst themselves and set borders to serve their own interests. In Berlin, Germany, in 1884–1885, the major European powers, without the knowledge or participation of the African leaders or peoples, carved up African empires, kingdoms, and other political communities into separate entities under European flags, sometimes dividing peoples that were ethnically and culturally united, sometimes uniting people who were historic rivals, and sometimes dividing larger political units that controlled routes and various resources. When Africans fought to keep their territories intact, wars followed, and many people were killed. At independence, colonies became states within the borders the colonizers had created.

Realizing that these artificial borders would create future problems for the newly independent states, President Nkrumah of Ghana and President Sekou Toure of Guinea became co-presidents of their respective countries in 1959 in a unique attempt to lessen the tension over European-imposed borders. Their agreement was also unique because Ghana had been a British colony and Guinea a French colony—the two had been kept separate prior to independence. The co-presidency ended with the overthrow of Nkrumah in a military coup in 1966. Julius Nyerere took a different approach to the border problem. He had taught biology and English in the British colony of Tanganyika and became active in the struggle against colonial rule. After Tanganyika gained independence in 1961, Nyerere was elected president. In 1964, he formed a union with the island country of Zanzibar and created the country now known as Tanzania.

One of the main themes of the OAU's Charter concerned the territorial integrity of national frontiers. The OAU founders vowed to respect the boundaries of existing states; they believed the Europeans had meddled with pre-existing boundaries and arrangements and were determined not to act in the same overbearing way the colonialists had. Nor did the OAU want to encourage the breakup of the new and fragile states.

CREATING DEMOCRACY

The early days of independence were full of hope and optimism in most African countries, but internal divisions were obvious even among the groups that had fought for their freedom. There were also great needs and demands from the expectant populations. New leaders tended to respond by centralizing political power and limiting opposition parties. They tried to expand the state organizations they had inherited from the colonizers, and they built large armies. By the late 1960s, many African states were ruled by one party, which rewarded its supporters and suppressed competition. As the armed forces became more powerful, though, many countries experienced military coups in which officers overthrew civilian governments. A few regimes engaged in brutal human rights abuses. There was limited investment in basic services or new industry.

The OAU Charter had included a principle of nonintervention in the member states' internal affairs—in other words, the organization would not tell members what they should do in terms of politics or economics. In the OAU's early years, leaders debated about whether they should allow military leaders who had overthrown civilian governments to join the organization. They decided to recognize whoever held power. The OAU was also ineffective in addressing human rights abuses. For example, during Idi Amin's reign of terror in Uganda, the OAU was not only silent about the abuse but elected the dictator chair of the organization.

Nevertheless, governments did take an interest in politics beyond their own borders. In the 1960s, decolonization was not yet complete and wars of liberation were being waged. The first generation of post-independence leaders supported liberation movements. As civil wars occurred within countries and weakened states, it was tempting for rulers in neighboring states to become involved. Border wars between Ivory Coast and Ghana, Nigeria and Cameroon, the Congo and its neighbors were frequently rooted in competition for resources and international trade. Many border wars erupted between nations that had been divided by the colonizers.

Since its founding, the AU has tried to insist upon constitutional government—governments that follow laws written in their constitutions—for its members. The AU has also supported democracy, a form of constitutional government that gives power to a freely and fairly elected representative body. The case of Togo is a good example. In early 2005, the AU took action to support democracy in Togo after the death of Africa's longest-ruling dictator, Gnassingbe Eyadema.

Togo formed part of the Slave Coast, from which captives were shipped to the Americas by European slavers in the seventeenth century. In the 1880s, this area became a German colony, and it was later seized by Britain and France. France granted it independence in 1960, and Togo's first president was assassinated in a military coup three years later. The head of the armed forces, Gnassingbe Eyadema, seized power in a military coup in 1967 and dissolved all rival political parties. Even though political parties were technically allowed again in 1991, harassment of the opposition continued. When Gnassingbe Eyadema died in 2005 after 38 years in power, the military made his son, Faure Gnassingbe, president, instead of following the country's written constitution. It also sealed the borders to prevent the person who was meant to become the temporary president from returning to the country. Opposition leaders called on France and others to bring pressure on the government.

AU leaders condemned Togo's rulers. The Peace and Security Council voted to suspend Togo and called for the AU, Europe, and the UN immediately to ban travel for Togo's leaders, stop shipping arms there, and expel the country from the West African regional economic organization that is closely tied to the AU. They called what happened "a blatant and unacceptable violation of the Togolese Constitution." Fifteen thousand people stormed Lome, Togo's capital city, dancing, singing and playing drums.[13]

Three weeks after the violation of the Togolese Constitution, Faure Gnassingbe stepped down and Togo agreed to return to constitutional rule. Most observers said that the AU had played a critical role. The head of the Economic Community of West African States (ECOWAS) said, "We have demonstrated a capacity to solve our own problems. . . . Today we have made one step. We hope that we will continue to move forward in our efforts to bring democracy to our region." Olusegun Obasanjo, the former president of Nigeria, the most

When the long-serving dictator of Togo died, the military overtook the government and installed their own leaders instead of following their country's constitution, leading to protests and demonstrations. Fulfilling one of its main goals, the AU successfully pressured the Togolese military in 2005 to allow elections for a democratic government.

powerful country in West Africa, also personally played an important role.[14]

The Togolese people continued to struggle for democracy. Presidential elections in April 2005 were marked by violence. According to official results, Gnassingbe was elected with 60 percent of the vote. In October 2007, his ruling party won the elections to the country's Parliament, the legislative body. ECOWAS sent 100 election monitors, who said the elections were free, fair, and transparent. But the main opposition party claimed that fake election identification cards had been made and ballot boxes tampered with.[15]

PEACEKEEPING AND PEACEMAKING

From its founding, the OAU had as a guiding principle the peaceful settlement of all disputes by negotiation, mediation, conciliation, or arbitration. Yet given its respect for territorial integrity and noninterference in countries' internal affairs, the organization had difficulty helping to resolve problems inside countries or between two member states. For example, during the terrible civil war in Nigeria between 1967 and 1970, the OAU felt unable to intervene to protect the Igbo in eastern Nigeria, who were trying to establish their own state. The organization also was unable to resolve the wars between Ethiopia and Somalia. The issues in these countries defied peaceful solutions proposed by the OAU, which never had its own military force in any case.

Because the OAU was unable to intervene to settle conflicts in Africa, other organizations did so instead. Between 1960 and 1964, for example, the UN tried to make peace in the Congo, and it was involved in Somalia. Sometimes individual African countries acted on their own in trying to restore ousted governments or calm conflict.

In its brief six-year existence, the AU has had some successes in conflict resolution. In 2003, it deployed peacekeeping troops in Burundi and later successfully handed over the mission to the UN. The AU observed the cease-fire talks in Chad and participated in nation building in Somalia and in conflict resolution in Ivory Coast, the latter two countries in various stages of civil war.

The AU's response to the crisis in Darfur highlights its commitment to conflict resolution but also represents a daunting challenge. In 2003, terrible fighting erupted in Darfur in the western region of Sudan. The fighting was mainly between the government and government-backed Arab groups and non-Arab groups trying to hold on to their land and gain a voice in national politics. More recently the fighting has become a chaotic, confusing power struggle with dozens of

(continues on page 59)

Joined by UN peacekeeping forces in an effort to help maintain order and encourage peace in the region, the AU's peacekeepers in Darfur have received much-needed help and direction from their initial mission in the region. Since the AU started its operation in Darfur in 2004, rules and regulations have prevented their effectiveness, while also leading to the deaths of AU peacekeepers.

ISHMAEL BEAH, A CHILD SOLDIER

Ishmael Beah was born November 23, 1980, in Sierra Leone. He was one of the astounding numbers of African children forced into armed service. Several fighting factions in Africa have kidnapped or recruited children as soldiers over the past half century.

In January 1993, when Ishmael was 12, he set out from his town of Mogbwemo with his older brother and his friend Talloi for the town of Mattru Jong, where they planned to participate in a talent show. After the 16-mile walk, they arrived in Mattru Jong and met up with their friends, Gibrilla, Kaloko, and Khalilou.

The next day, the three friends whom Ishmael had met went to school but returned early. They reported that school had been canceled because rebels fighting against the government of Sierra Leone were probably coming to Mattru Jong, after already having attacked Ishmael's hometown nearby. Ishmael, his brother, and Talloi decided to return to their town to try to find their families. They passed parents screaming for their children and children crying for their parents traveling in opposite directions. Ishmael was warned against going back to town, but the three kept heading toward Mogbwemo. As they approached their home, Ishmael, his brother, and Talloi saw terrifying scenes. Parents were carrying their children, who had been shot dead by rebels. The parents were so grief-stricken and disoriented that they thought their children were still alive. Ishmael and his companions decided to return to Mattru Jong, because they realized that if their families were still in Mogbwemo they would be dead.

Ishmael, his brother, and Talloi began traveling with other refugees. They tried to avoid the rebels, but eventually they were captured. When the rebels attacked, the boys managed to escape in the confusion. They became separated, and Ishmael traveled by

Child soldiers have been used in wars and rebel groups in several African countries. Ishmael Beah, a former child soldier in Sierra Leone, was forced to fight and kill others until he was rescued by UNICEF. Here, Beah is holding the book he wrote about his life, *A Long Way Gone: Memoirs of a Boy Soldier*.

himself for days until eventually he joined another small group of boys. The new group continued to travel, avoiding the rebels and searching for their families. During the journey, Ishmael learned that his parents had been killed. Several of the boys died from illness during the trek. They were walking through the forest one day when they encountered a group of government soldiers fighting

(continues)

(continued)

rebels. The government soldiers gave them guns and made them fight, even though they were young children.

Ishmael has since said that during his time with the government soldiers, starting at the age of 13, he had killed more people than he could count. The child soldiers, including Ishmael, were kept high on marijuana and cocaine to numb them to killing. After three years of this hell, the United Nations Children's Fund (UNICEF) rescued Ishmael. While he was at a UNICEF center for child soldiers, he struggled with depression and other mental problems, resulting from all the brutalities he had witnessed and performed. Ishmael had been conditioned to feel that violence and brutality were normal and that people on the other side of the conflict were enemies to be hated and killed. Counselors helped him deal with these feelings. After showing progress, Ishmael went to live with his uncle in Freetown, the capital of Sierra Leone.

When rebels captured Freetown, Ishmael went to New York, where he met Laura Simms at a UN event for child soldiers and began to live with her. He finished high school in the United States and then studied at Oberlin College in Ohio. He became a prominent speaker at UN gatherings, and he currently works for the Children's Rights Division of Human Rights Watch. He also recently wrote a book about his life entitled *A Long Way Gone*. Hard as it is to believe, Ishmael Beah's story is similar to that of thousands of other young children caught up in African civil wars in such countries as Sudan, Liberia, Angola, Chad, the Democratic Republic of the Congo, Ivory Coast, Rwanda, Somalia, Uganda, Tanzania, and Sierra Leone.

—Written by Jonathan Bix, 15

(continued from page 54)

armed groups, an increase in banditry and violence, and even killing of peacekeepers. Since the outbreak of violence in 2003, about 200,000 people have been killed and 2.5 million people have been displaced. One of the key challenges to peace in the region concerns control of the abundant oil reserves in the southern region of Darfur and the area surrounding them. Like many of Africa's natural resources, oil reserves in Sudan, Nigeria, Guinea Bissau, and now Ghana are sparking civil wars and magnifying many humanitarian crises. After an April 2004 cease-fire agreement in Darfur, the AU took a leading role in observing the situation, but both the fighting and humanitarian problems continued. The AU expanded its mission to about 3,300 soldiers who would protect civilians and monitor the cease-fire. In 2005, it expanded its force to about 7,000, but this number was insufficient to maintain the cease-fire and protect civilians.

In August 2007, UN Resolution 1769 authorized for Darfur the world's largest peacekeeping operation costing about $2 billion in its first year and drawing upon about 26,000 military and police forces from both the AU and the UN. The chair of the African Union Commission held talks with Sudanese President Omar al-Bashir and said that the force would be drawn from African countries and under African command. This was partly a way to reassure the Sudanese president that African authority would remain strong and the area would not be overrun by foreign troops, and it was in keeping with the AU's interest in Africans resolving problems on their own continent. The commander appointed by the AU is General Martin Agwai. Sudan agreed to accept the force, and troops, mainly from African countries, were deployed without further restrictions from the Sudanese government.

At the beginning of October 2007, rebels attacked a small peacekeeping base in Darfur, killing 10 peacekeepers from three African countries, making it more difficult to raise the new peacekeeping troops. The AU force had already suffered deaths, and President Abdoulaye of Senegal threatened to pull out his 538 troops unless they were adequately equipped to defend themselves. Senegal had pledged to increase its commitment to 1,600 troops. Nigeria had the largest number of troops in Darfur and was also concerned.[16]

In October 2007, the Sudanese government declared a unilateral cease-fire, but key rebel leaders boycotted the peace talks. This terrible conflict remains unresolved, in military, political, and humanitarian terms, but the AU, the UN, and many world leaders are working toward a solution.[17]

Another example of the African Union's active involvement in the political affairs of member states occurred during the Liberian crisis. The AU spent many months negotiating the end of President Charles Taylor's rule after he was indicted for war crimes by a UN court in Sierra Leone, a country that borders Liberia. Taylor was accused of selling arms for diamonds to Liberian rebels and of fueling a brutal fourteen-year civil war in his own country as well. He was charged with forcing children to fight as soldiers in the civil war. In all, more than 300,000 people died as a result of these actions.[18] Taylor currently awaits trial at the International Court of Justice in The Hague, Netherlands. In 2005, Ellen Johnson-Sirleaf was elected President of Liberia, the first female president of an African nation.

The AU and
African Economies

EUROPEAN COLONIALISM DISRUPTED TRADITIONAL AFRICAN economies, and as colonies began to assert their desire for independence, they prepared long-term economic development plans and were optimistic that they could achieve rapid economic growth. But this did not happen. The physical infrastructure—such as railways, roads, and electricity and telephone lines—was poor and had been created to benefit the colonizers' economies. It needed to be re-created almost from scratch. There were few universal educational systems, and the number of Africans training in technology, business, or public management was insufficient. African economies continued to be dependent upon exports of single crops or minerals, leaving them at the mercy of global demand and prices for those goods, and large foreign companies dominated production in many countries.

There was some overall growth in African economies after 1960, but the growth has varied by country and did not always mean that people were doing well. If the wealthy few control the resources and reap the benefits of economic growth, the poor see little or no benefit. Economic growth must also be understood in relation to population growth; there were countries in Africa where the populations grew faster than the economies. Also, growth often came at the expense of significant environmental degradation—polluted water and soil and disfigured land—due to lack of government regulation. This is one of the problems with oil production in the Niger Delta in Nigeria, where environmental degradation threatens the livelihoods of people who have lived there for thousands of years. Other development burdens included natural disasters and tropical diseases.

Today, most observers would say, sub-Saharan Africa is in an economic crisis involving weak agriculture, little industry, lack of control over export prices, high levels of debt to other countries, poor conditions of life for ordinary people, environmental destruction, and the HIV/AIDS pandemic and other illnesses. Poverty is wide and very deep. According to the World Bank, a greater proportion of people in Africa than anywhere else (46 percent) live in poverty, and the total number of people living on less than one dollar per day is about 291 million.[19]

The AU aims to improve African economies and recapture the continent's economic position in the world trading system for the benefit of its people. It goes about this in several ways. As the OAU, it had tried to encourage economic integration (creating closer economic ties and lowering barriers to trading and movement across state borders) of the sub-Saharan regions and the continent as a whole. More recently, as the AU, it has been closely associated with an economic plan called the New Partnership for Africa's Development, or NEPAD. In addition, it focuses on the basic things all economies need to thrive, such as an educated population.

Because 46 percent of Africa's population live in poverty, many of them cannot afford adequate housing or basic services. The continent's largest slum, Kibera *(above)*, is estimated to house 600,000 Kenyans in tin-roof shacks without running water, waste management, or health care. The government claims they are unable to help due to the enormous debts they owe to foreign countries.

ECONOMIC INTEGRATION

The AU believes that the economic integration of its member states—efforts by separate countries to unify their economies—gives the continent the ability to grow, modernize, and trade. Such efforts include lowering tariffs, taxes on goods coming in from other countries; creating common standards for what can be traded (for example, requiring food to be free of certain pesticides); coordinating and linking their transportation systems; and perhaps creating a single currency, like the euro, to be used in more than one country.

There are many arguments for economic integration, especially in Africa. Working together on railways, roadways, and other transportation structures uses scarce resources for the benefit of several economies. Investing together in training and education raises the level of the workforce. In countries with small economies, integration makes a wider range of goods and materials available to meet the populations' needs and for manufacturing. African companies, especially in cases where it is difficult to compete in global trade and sell agricultural goods on other continents, can find markets on their own huge continent. With bigger markets, companies can grow larger and more competitive. Integrated economies might also be more attractive to foreign investors and be able to speak with one voice in international trade negotiations.

Like leaders in other regions of the world, some African leaders believe that to help economies grow, it is better to lower barriers to trade between countries than put tariffs on exports and imports between them. Countries have different natural, human, and capital resources and ways of combining these. When regions and countries specialize in what they can produce at the lowest cost and then trade, everyone's production and consumption of goods will increase. Also, when countries cooperate and are interdependent economically, they may be less likely to go to war.

The drive toward economic integration on the continent began under the OAU. Although the OAU focused mainly on political unity, it also helped develop regional economic communities beginning in the 1960s. In 1991 it established the African Economic Community to unify the regional economic communities such as the Economic Community of West African States (ECOWAS) and the Southern African Development Community (SADC), so that they could negotiate international trade and development agreements. This strategy called for creating an economically unified continent built on the economic integration that was already underway in the regions.

The African Economic Community unites about 14 economic communities, corresponding to the geographic regions of Africa, with different kinds of economic cooperation in place. Some countries belong to more than one of these groups. Leaders of the regional economic communities are generally highly knowledgeable about their regions. They are economists, entrepreneurs, trade union representatives, researchers, educators, and others. They focus on expanding trade among the member states of each particular region and between regions of Africa. A large part of their mission is the coordination of natural and human resources. They are intent on improving the educational level of their most vulnerable and uneducated citizens, and they try to match training and education to the specific needs of the economy.

One of the strongest regional communities is ECOWAS, established in 1975. In their treaty, 15 West African states

THE MAIN REGIONAL ECONOMIC COMMUNITIES IN AFRICA

The Economic Community of West African States (ECOWAS)	Benin, Burkina Faso, Cape Verde, Ivory Coast, the Gambia, Ghana, Guinea, Guinea Bissau, Liberia, Mali, Niger, Nigeria, Senegal, Sierra Leone, and Togo
The Southern African Development Community (SADC)	Angola, Botswana, Democratic Republic of the Congo, Lesotho, Malawi, Mauritius, Mozambique, Namibia, Seychelles, South Africa, Swaziland, Tanzania, Zambia, Zimbabwe.
The Common Market for Eastern and Southern Africa (COMESA)	Burundi, Comoros, DR Congo, Djibouti, Egypt, Eritrea, Ethiopia, Kenya, Madagascar, Malawi, Mauritius, Rwanda, Seychelles, Swaziland, Sudan, Uganda, Zambia, Zimbabwe
The Economic Community of Central African States (ECCAS)	Angola, Burundi, Cameroon, Central African Republic, Chad, DR Congo, Guinea, Gabon, Rwanda, Sao Tome, and Principe
The Arab Mahgreb Union (UMA)	Algeria, Libya, Morocco, Mauritania, Tunisia

agreed to try to increase trade among them and to establish a special bank for the region. In the 1970s and 1980s, ECOWAS countries also agreed to support each other if there were threats from the outside and to take action if there were serious internal conflicts threatening the region's stability. They pledged to uphold democracy and the rule of law. ECOWAS has a peacekeeping force and has been active in trying to resolve conflicts in Sierra Leone, Guinea Bissau, and Liberia.

There are different opinions as to how well these regional economic communities have been working, what more they might do, and how they can lead to more continent-wide economic integration. Many commentators contend that there are too many groups and that conflicts multiply when countries belong to more than one. Others worry that creating trade without tariffs in these groups eliminates import taxes and so depletes the revenue available to governments to provide services to their populations. Still others want the African Economic Community to encourage these regional groups to set the same priorities and rules. Whatever their promise of advancement, some economists say, the level of trade within these smaller communities remains disappointingly uneven.

NEPAD

African leaders have been exploring how to solve the problem of Africa's low level of economic wealth and ability to meet its population's needs since independence. In 2001, at the final OAU summit, leaders introduced a plan that is now referred to as the New Partnership for Africa's Development (NEPAD). NEPAD's official main objectives are to eliminate poverty in Africa, put African countries on a path to continuing economic development, bring Africa into the global economy in a positive way, and empower women in African societies.

NEPAD believes that the reasons Africa has failed to grow economically are its lack of sound democracy, peace and security, and honest and strong governments. Leaders consider it essential that Africa attract investment from overseas partners, both governments and companies, but it is difficult to do this where there is corruption, civil war, and military rule. NEPAD suggests the necessity of good government and democracy as a condition for economic growth. At the Durban Summit in July 2002, the Assembly of Heads of State and Government issued a Declaration on Democracy, Political, Economic and Corporate Governance. According to this declaration, states participating in NEPAD "believe in just, honest, transparent, accountable, and participatory government and probity in public life."[20] Member countries are expected to enforce the rule of law, equality before the law, individual and collective freedoms, the right to participate in the democratic process, and separation of powers of the executive, the legislature, and an independent judiciary. The AU set up a procedure, called the African Peer Review Mechanism, where countries would check on each other's compliance with these standards, using peer pressure to get countries to improve their institutions and behaviors.

Building on the work of other groups, NEPAD argues that the debt that African countries owe should be reduced or entirely forgiven. African debt amounts to about $200 billion, and Africa spends $14 billion paying back each year. This diverts money from basic human needs and services, such as health care and education, and makes it difficult for Africa to promote economic development. NEPAD has drawn up a process for reviewing whether countries' debts can be forgiven, erased completely, or changed to make them less of a burden. But if a debt is modified, the benefits must go to education, health, and training.

Because NEPAD recognizes the problem of lack of infrastructure—roadways, railroads, ports, power generators, and water—it emphasizes the importance of focusing on these projects. And because these projects are expensive, it seeks commitments from outside.

(continues on page 70)

CAN SOCCER HELP AFRICAN ECONOMIES?

"A food pot is symbolic in Africa," Danny Jordan, a World Cup organizer explained. "It's about sharing; everybody eating together out of the same pot."* He was discussing the design of one of the new soccer stadiums, resembling an earthenware food pot, being built near Johannesburg for the 2010 World Cup. The matches will be played at 10 stadiums across nine South African cities, including Johannesburg, the wealthiest province in South Africa, and Capetown, the law-making capital of South Africa. Five of the stadiums are being improved, and five stadiums are being constructed from scratch. Each stadium will have the capacity to seat 40,000 to 70,000 people.

Not only stadiums but also public transportation needs to be boosted in the run-up to the tournament. The government of South Africa has said that it will fund most of the major building related to the tournament, but one study calculated that the event would contribute about 21 billion rand, the South African currency, to the economy as a whole, create more tax income for the government, and create about 150,000 jobs, leaving behind much better tourist, communications, and transportation structures.**

Football, as soccer is called in Africa, is the continent's leading sport, played by professionals and amateurs, by young people and adults, on dirt lots, on soccer fields, and in modern stadiums. Fans watch games on televisions in homes, bars and restaurants, public squares in the middle of big cities, and even hospitals. Skilled African teams are a great source of national pride and passion, and are organized within the Confederation of African Football. One of Africa's most famous exports is soccer stars—Samuel Eto'o from Cameroon who plays for Barcelona, Liberia's George Weah who played for Chelsea and AC Milan, Didier Drogba from Ivory Coast who played for Chelsea. George Weah is a devoted humanitarian, a founder of a youth football team in Monrovia that emphasizes the importance of school and sports, and a former candidate for the presidency of Liberia in 2005.

FIFA (Federation Internationale de Football Association), the international association that organizes world soccer, accepted South Africa's bid to host the 2010 World Cup, after South Africa showed that it had the ability to host the games and accommodate players, spectators, and world media. It will be the first time this major tournament between the world's top 32 national soccer teams will be played on the continent of Africa. While the 2010 World Cup will be in South Africa, President Thabo Mbeki has declared the 2010 World Cup an African, not just a South African, event. Even more, he has declared it an event for Africans living all around the world.

In the run-up to the 2010 World Cup, the AU declared 2007 The International Year of African Football. This special year was launched at the 8th African Union Summit. Fifteen-year-old players from Ethiopia and South Africa and African soccer stars Lausha Bwalya and Abed Pele of Ghana participated in the launch.

The AU celebrates the sport as a way of improving health, focusing on young people, reducing poverty, creating jobs, and getting all levels of society to work together—families, communities, clubs, leagues, youth sports associations, professional soccer teams, private businesses, and political leaders. It is seen as having an important role in achieving NEPAD economic development objectives.

* Xan Rice, "Ready or Not," *Observer*, June 3, 2007. Available online at *http://football.guardian.co.uk/print/0,,329948830-103,00.html*.

** T.T. Mboweni, "The Benefits of Being a Good Host: The FIFA World Cup and the South African Economy," 20 March 2007. Available online at *www.reservebank.co.za/internet/publication.nsf*.

(continued from page 67)

HOW NATURAL RESOURCES
AFFECT AFRICA'S ECONOMIES

Natural resources are elements that are considered useful or valuable in their naturally occurring form. These include such basic things as water and sunlight, but also materials that need to be extracted from the ground and/or purified, like oil, diamonds, or copper. Natural resources are critical components of all economies and the countries of Africa are rich in them. Whether a society benefits from such resources depends not upon how much of a resource exists but upon how that resource is managed and extracted, and who benefits from its use or sale. In the colonial period, the presence of resources created little prosperity and development for Africans but contributed to the profits of large European mining companies, manufacturers, and merchants. The leadership of the AU, with its focus upon good governance and economic development, is aware of the complexities of the extraction and use of natural resources, and it seeks to establish new ways of working with those who want and need the continent's riches.

Water

Water is not only essential to human life and health but also to sustainable agriculture and other industrial processes. Africa has only nine percent of the world's fresh water but about 20 percent of the world's population. And the water resources it has are distributed unevenly across the continent. Only 64 percent of the population has access to treated water, and less than half of people living in cities have clean water. In Africa, extreme drought and other disasters create water emergencies. Agriculture uses 88 percent of the water in Africa, making irrigation a high priority for many African countries. The World Watch Institute says that it takes 1,000 tons of water to produce a ton of grain, which makes importing grain to Africa more effective than importing water—not that this option is available to poor countries, even though few of them can afford to

Lack of water has been a reason to start conflict in the past, and African countries, as well as the AU, have made efforts to improve water management and distribute resources throughout the continent to both ordinary people and farmers. South Africa, for example, has greatly increased distribution to black townships and is trying to create more accessible water resources for the remaining 7 million South Africans who need this basic service.

invest in working irrigation systems or even to repair leaky pipes that carry water to families. Large dams that generate electricity can be counterproductive—they keep water out of circulation downstream from the dam, and deprive downstream farmers, households, and fisheries of water and livelihoods. Water experts predict that the main conflicts in Africa over the next 25 years could be over rights to water, especially where rivers and lakes are shared by more than one country—around the Nile, Niger, Volta, and Zambezi river basins.[21]

Water scarcity in apartheid South Africa, for example, was aggravated by political decisions that affected the majority black population, leaving about one-third of the population living in the segregated black communities without access to safe water. When the African National Congress came to power in 1994, access to water was declared a basic human right. Since then, South Africa has achieved remarkable progress in expanding access to clean water—it took 10 years, but by 2004, about 88 percent of the population had access to clean water. However, problems remain. In South Africa after apartheid, private water companies may charge even the very poor for water and sometimes require people to pre-pay before giving them access to safe drinking water. In some places, companies also installed special devices called tricklers to slow the flow of water through delivery pipes.

Avoiding conflict over water resources and distributing adequate water to both households and farmers is a major concern of the AU, which has established an African Ministerial Council on Water (AMCOW), described as "the highest level water policy-making body on the continent" to address water problems before they reach a crisis point. All African ministers with responsibility for water resources belong to the council. The mission of AMCOW is to provide political leadership, policy direction, and government cooperation, as well as financing the development of interconnected water supplies, which is a serious economic problem because it requires materials and skilled technicians. Financing the distribution of freshwater facilities is very costly, according to Peter Akari, chief water policy officer of the African Water Facility at the African Development Bank. It requires financial assistance from a variety of partners in building infrastructure.[22]

Oil

While many people are aware that the Middle Eastern countries of Saudi Arabia, Iran, and Iraq have large quantities of oil, the African continent holds 10 percent to 12 percent of the world's known oil reserves. Oil is found mainly in Nigeria, the world's eleventh largest producer, at about 2.5 billion barrels a day. Other countries with oil reserves include Angola, Sudan, Equatorial Guinea, Gabon, and the Congo. Nigeria is the fifth largest supplier of oil to the United States, and Sudan supplies an increasing percentage of China's imported oil.[23]

Most of Nigeria's oil reserves are in the Niger Delta. A journalist who has studied the delta says, "People there live almost as if it's the Stone Age. They live in stick huts on little islands in the mangrove swamps. Many of the villages are accessible only by boat. Nearby, you will have these multi-billion-dollar oil facilities, with executives being dropped in by helicopter. A thousand people a year are killed in small-scale guerilla warfare in the [d]elta. Boys drill holes in the pipelines at night and suck out the oil. . . . The money is siphoned off to arm the guerilla groups."[24] Offshore oil refineries also create problems for the fishing communities that live along the Western Africa shoreline. While the Nigerian state gets about 70 percent of its revenues from oil, poverty in Nigeria remains.

Is oil a blessing or a curse in Africa? According to many commentators, oil is often a curse. If a country discovers oil, the value of its currency goes up, making its other exports more expensive and harder to sell. Moreover, workers may migrate to booming oil areas, leaving behind farms and other industries. After oil was discovered in Nigeria in 1957, the country changed from an agricultural to an oil-dependent economy and now has to import its food. Because the government gets a great deal of income from oil, it may not work as hard to diversify the economy by creating new industries or to educate its population. The oil money seldom gets to the people, but it lines the pockets of the powerful and the already rich. The oil companies themselves put their profits first and tend to develop close relationships with authoritarian rulers who will do their bidding.

The AU does not govern the oil industry directly or set rules about how states should relate to large private oil companies. In

One of the growing concerns of the AU stems from the involvement of the large, international oil companies in Africa. Because of the continent's oil reserves, the people who run the oil companies are profiting from the oil sales, while bribing leaders and governments to act in their favor. Oil facilities, like this Nigerian one, rarely benefit African citizens or local economies.

fact, different countries in Africa have different relationships with oil companies and different ways of claiming revenues from oil discovered on their lands or in their waters. However, the AU is concerned with issues related both directly and indirectly to oil: agricultural sustainability, transparent government, education and training of the population, democratic practices and human rights, and an end to civil violence. Also, if African countries, including the non-oil producers, are going to develop, they need access to oil, an expensive commodity. The AU is trying to arrange for help from oil producers for non-producers so that all countries in Africa have access to this important resource. At the same time, the AU views solar, wind, and hydroelectric power as alternative energy resources that offer promise, especially for rural communities.

GLOBAL TRADE

Since independence African countries have been struggling to gain benefits from a global trading and economic system that stacks the odds against it. Africa's share of world trade actually fell from 6 percent in 1980 to about 2 percent ten years later. In 2005, most of sub-Saharan Africa's exports went to European countries (34.4%), the United States (29.6%), and China (10.9%). Imports include 31.3 percent from Europe and 5.9 percent from the United States. African countries still export mainly raw commodities—fruit, vegetables, flowers, oil, diamonds, gold, and copper.[25] Many political leaders in Africa believe that an increase in exports would help African economies grow, and for this, cooperation with wealthier countries remains urgent.

African leaders have been arguing for many years that new rules set by the World Trade Organization (WTO) and their enforcement must be fair, if African countries are to develop. While on the whole NEPAD and the ministers of trade favor an open trading approach, they insist on having some control over their fragile economies.

(continues on page 78)

FAIR TRADE FOR AFRICAN COTTON GROWERS

In Koulikoro, Mali, in West Africa, Seydou Coulibaly used to be able to support his family—a wife, six children, and two brothers—by growing cotton. For the past six years, though, he has had trouble. "I have struggled to make enough money to feed and clothe my family because of the price of cotton on the world market. Agricultural policies developed for farmers in the [United States] hurt us on the other side of the globe. In my village, we have difficulties paying for the costs of basic education, health care, and even drinkable water. We used to have six teachers in the village . . . [but] we had to let three go. We never had a doctor in the village, but we used to have a nurse and a midwife. We could only afford to pay one, so we had to let the nurse go. There are five water pumps, but three of them are broken and we do not have the means to fix them. So we are left to share two in the whole village, among people and animals."*

When AU leaders demand fair trade for Africa, they usually mean creating and enforcing world trade rules (set by the WTO) that allow Africa to do more to ensure its own success and rely less on aid from wealthy countries. They point to United States and European government subsidies to crops like cotton as examples of unfair trade. Giving subsidies to cotton farmers in the United States allows them to produce more. Then they sell what is not bought in the United States at low prices abroad. This lowers the price of cotton around the world and thus the income for cotton producers in poorer African countries, which cannot afford to give their farmers subsidies. "There is no point in giving with one hand and taking with the other," then-UN Secretary-General Kofi Annan told the World Food Summit in June 2002, commenting on the impact of subsidies on agricultural products in the rich world. "You put yourself in the shoes of a

Put in place to benefit farmers in the United States, American subsidies place another obstacle in the path of economic and agricultural development in Africa, as climate change and corruption threatens the livelihood of cotton growers and pickers throughout the continent.

small developing country which cannot export its agricultural products because of restrictions and tariffs, a small developing country cannot compete on the world market."**

More than 10 million people in West and Central Africa rely upon exported cotton for their livelihoods. Many of these countries are mono-crop economies, depending upon one crop for earnings. But experts say that U.S. cotton subsidies have pushed down prices of cotton around the world so that growers in Africa earn less than they could if there were no subsidies. Studies show

(continues)

(continued)

that between 2001 and 2005, cotton growers in the African countries of Benin, Burkina Faso, Chad, and Mali have lost about $328
million because of U.S. subsidies.

Countries in Latin America and Africa have been protest-
ing these subsidies, and the WTO ruled in 2007 that U.S. cotton
subsidies were illegal. In October 2007, cotton-industry officials in
Burkina Faso, Africa's largest cotton producer, expressed hope that
their dire situation would improve: "I am hopeful that the situation here will get better," said the president of the African Cotton
Producers Association, Francois Traore. "It tells the truth that there
are distortions against Africa's development interest. Subsidies are
preventing us from living," he added. "If nothing is done, we can say
that nobody wants us to develop."***

---

* "Fields of Hope: African Farmers Tell Their Stories." Available online at
*http://www.oxfam.america.org/whatwedo/campaigns/agriculture/news_publica-
tions/fields_of_hope/index_html.*

** Gumisai Mutume, "Mounting Opposition to Northern Farm Subsidies,"
Africa Recovery, Vol. 17, No. 1, May 2003. Available online at
http:// www.un.org/ecosocdev/geninfo/afrec/vol17no1/171agri4.htm.

*** "Burkina Faso: Cotton Producers Celebrate WTO Ruling Against U.S.
Subsidies." Available online at *http://www.irnnews.org.*

(continued from page 75)

The rules about agriculture are especially important, given
the fact that so much of Africa and so many of its poorest
people produce agricultural products. African leaders feel
that rich countries follow a double standard: They tell African
countries they cannot subsidize their farmers or industries,
but the rich countries themselves, including those in Europe

and the United States, have subsidies. In particular, the United States and European countries subsidize their agriculture in a way that destroys the livelihoods of some African producers. African trade ministers have opposed the U.S. payments of subsidies to American cotton farmers, lowering the world price of cotton and driving African cotton farmers out of business. Similarly the EU subsidizes sugar-beet farmers, even though it would be cheaper to make sugar from African sugarcane. African leaders have asked the WTO to rule that these are unfair subsidies, according to its own rules.

African Union ministers also oppose rules that would force them to cut all their tariffs on imports, since many of their industries, in clothing and fishing, for example, are vulnerable. Finally, they oppose a world body telling them how they should deliver services, including health care, to their populations—an area covered by ongoing WTO negotiations. They have benefited from preferences extended to their economies by some countries, including the EU and the United States, and worry that new WTO rules might remove these.

In February 1999, the United States passed a law called the African Growth and Opportunity Act (AGOA) that the U.S. government said would help African trade. The basic idea behind the act was that if African countries took down some of their barriers to U.S. businesses and U.S. exports entering their countries, the United States would make it easier for African goods to enter the large U.S. market. The act stated that the United States would extend duty-free (no tariff) treatment to many sub-Saharan African countries and eliminate existing quotas (limits on imports) on textile and clothing imports from Kenya and Mauritius under certain conditions. While many people welcomed this act, others said that it emphasized trade at the expense of development assistance to Africa and denied power to African leaders to control their own economies.

When the U.S. government reported on the results of the AGOA in 2007, they said that trade between the United States and sub-Saharan African countries increased 17 percent in 2006 over 2005, reaching almost $71.3 billion, with both U.S. exports to and U.S. imports from the region growing. "The [a]dministration is proud of its efforts to bring sub-Saharan Africa more fully into the community of trading nations. Trade is the best tool we have to alleviate poverty and spur economic development, and AGOA is a key element in America's effort," said U.S. Trade Representative Susan C. Schwab. "Since AGOA's launch in 2000, two-way trade between the United States and sub-Saharan African countries has increased 143 percent."[26]

The AU and Society

THE AU IS AN ORGANIZATION OF GOVERNMENTS, BUT ONE that aspires to understand and value the everyday life of people on the continent and to draw ordinary people and their civil society organizations into the life of the AU. The AU has numerous ways to find out about people's needs, and it works on many areas of social needs and culture. It has also set up a special organ, the Economic, Social and Cultural Council (ECOSOCC), in which civil society organizations—groups that work on matters of urgent and everyday public concern but are not part of governments—are directly represented.

The AU is interested not only in unifying the political leaders and economies of Africa, it is also interested in creating links across national boundaries to unify the African continent at the grassroots level. The AU civil society organizations focus on young people hoping for a good future; activists fighting to protect the environment; doctors, nurses, and others wanting to improve health care for all; and teachers who think that adults as well as children should have a chance to get an education. It is also interested in strengthening a culture of participation.

THE ECOSOCC

The Economic, Social and Cultural Council was created as a people-centered rather than government-centered organ of the AU, whose task it is to coordinate and encourage the efforts of civil society in Africa. Wangari Maathai, professor, 2004 Nobel Peace Prize winner, and president of ECOSOCC, explains, "The distinctive character of the African Union's ECOSOCC is that it is an opportunity for African civil society to play an active role in charting the future of the continent, organizing itself in partnership with African governments to contribute to the principles, policies, and programs of the Union."[27]

Civil society organizations (CSOs) work directly with people and often aim to influence public policies, opening up new forms of participation for citizens. In the United States, parent-teacher organizations, ecology centers, labor unions, the NAACP, and the American Civil Liberties Union (ACLU) are examples of civil society organizations. The CSOs that operate throughout Africa also help create or strengthen civic participation. The Treatment Action Campaign in South Africa, for example, is a civil society organization that campaigns for treatment of people with HIV and to reduce new infections. The Pan-African Association for Literacy and Adult Education argues that people should have access to learning to read and basic education across their lifetimes, even when they are adults. The Green Belt Movement of

Many civil society organizations are involved in grassroots campaigns to help African citizens feel more involved with their government, as well as helping them gain control of their local environment and rights. The ECOSOCC helps connect the participants in civil society organizations with the operations of the AU, making both parties more accountable for their activities and more accessible for advice.

Kenya works on protecting the environment and planting trees to improve the ecology of Kenya, as well as on the rights of women and girls.

Civil society organizations are especially important in Africa, given the low levels of people's participation in their governments in some countries and the important roles such organizations play in promoting democratic government, human rights, peace, and social progress. Through ECOSOCC, people can be closer to the center of what the AU is doing and so make the AU itself more accountable.

Colonialism exaggerated the breach between various groups within Africa, such as the Western- and non-Western edu- cated, literate and illiterate, men and women, and others. ECOSOCC is a way in which people can overcome these divi- sions by uniting behind common goals and strategies.

The ECOSOCC advises other bodies of the AU but is most closely linked to the commission. It is also designed to promote a common AU vision and build bridges between governments and civil society. Its membership is particularly focused on women, youth, civic organizations, and the private sector. It seeks the participation and expertise of the African diaspora in strengthening the AU mission, goals, and civil organizations. According to its statutes, or governing policies, ECOSOCC has the authority to put AU programs and policies into practice. Civil society organizations that become certified members must actively promote peace, security, and stability in Africa. They must engage in the creation of a culture of good gover- nance among its citizens.

The ECOSOCC is structured to cover a range of important issues where civil society organizations are active. There are 10 cluster committees, each focused on one theme.

Who are the members of the ECOSOCC? There are 150 representatives of civil society organizations, including differ- ent social and professional groups in member states and in the diaspora. Two CSOs from each member country have seats. Ten regional and eight continent-wide CSOs are represented. Twenty CSOs from the African diaspora outside the conti- nent have seats. According to Article Four of the ECOSOCC's statute, 50 percent of the council's representatives must be women and 50 percent must be between the ages of 18 and 35. ECOSOCC also promotes membership among the disabled, senior citizens, labor unions, nongovernmental organizations such as professional organizations, cultural organizations, and organizations for people with special needs.

(continues on page 88)

THE TEN SECTORAL CLUSTER COMMITTEES OF ECOSOCC

ESTABLISHED TO FORMULATE OPINIONS AND PROVIDE INPUT INTO THE POLICIES AND PROGRAMS OF THE AFRICAN UNION[28]

Peace and Security	conflict anticipation; prevention; management and resolution; post-conflict reconstruction and peace building; prevention and combating of terrorism; use of child soldiers; drug trafficking; illicit proliferation of small arms and light weapons; and security reforms, etc.
Political Affairs	human rights; rule of law; democratic and constitutional rule; good governance; power-sharing; electoral institutions; humanitarian affairs and assistance, etc.
Infrastructure and Energy	energy; transport; communications; infrastructure; and tourism, etc.
Social Affairs and Health	health; children; drug control; population; migration; labor and employment; family; aging; the physically challenged; sports; culture; youth; and protection and social integration, etc.
Human Resources, Science and Technology	education; illiteracy; information technology; communication; human resources; science and technology, etc.
Trade and Industry	trade; industry; handicrafts; customs and immigration matters, etc.
Rural Economy and Agriculture	rural economy; agriculture and food security; livestock; environment; water and natural resources; and desertification, etc.
Economic Affairs	economic integration; monetary and financial affairs; private-sector development, including the informal sector; and resource mobilization, etc.
Women and Gender	women; gender and development as a crosscutting issue, etc.
Cross-Cutting Programs	all other cross-cutting issues that are not covered in above clusters, including HIV/AIDS, international cooperation, coordination with institutions and organs of the Union

WANGARI MAATHAI AND
THE GREEN BELT MOVEMENT

Forests all over Africa are at risk. In Africa as a whole, half of all forests have been cut within the past hundred years. In Kenya, the tree cover is only 30 percent of what it once was—only 2 percent of land is forested.[*] The loss of forests in Kenya has occurred for many reasons. Some cut trees to grow coffee and tea profitably. Others logged for the timber. Still others cleared forests for human settlement and agriculture, especially as Kenya's population grew. And people with no other source of fuel cut firewood for energy.

The destruction of forests have devastating consequences. The removal of trees leads to loss of topsoil, making land less useful for growing food as well as prone to flooding. "Losing topsoil should be compared to losing territories to an invading enemy," Wangari Maathai says. If African countries were so threatened they would mobilize their armies, the police, the reserves—even citizens would be called to fight."[**] In partnership with the National Council of Women of Kenya, Maathai organized the Green Belt Movement (GBM) to reduce the effects of deforestation and provide a way for women to be effective leaders, while raising public awareness of the ecological crisis. The project started by planting trees on private lands when owners are willing. Now the Green Belt Movement monitors the grabbing of public land, destruction of forests, poor governance, and abuse of people's rights. It also plants trees on public lands. At the same time, the project educates children and adults about the importance of trees and soil conservation.

Women collect seeds from the existing forest and plant them in nurseries, sometimes supplementing them with seeds supplied by various organizations. Once trees begin to grow from the seedlings, they are transplanted into individual containers or plastic bags. When these young plants are ready to be distributed, the groups

Through her work with the Green Belt Movement, activist Wangari Maathai *(left)* has developed an organization that encourages Africans to maintain peace, responsible governments, and environmental protection through the planting of trees. For her work, Maathai won the Nobel Peace Prize in 2004.

tell their communities and ask those interested to dig and prepare the holes, or they plant on public lands to reforest and preserve biological diversity. Group members check the holes to make sure they are dug correctly, distribute and plant the seedlings, and check on growing trees. Women receive some pay for their work.

Born in Nyeri, Kenya, in 1940, the daughter of farmers in the highlands of Mount Kenya, Wangari Maathai won the 2004 Nobel Peace Prize "for her contribution to sustainable development, democracy, and peace." She went to school in Kansas, earned

(continues)

(continued)

a master's degree in Pennsylvania, and pursued a doctorate in Germany, earning her Ph.D. from the University of Nairobi, where she taught veterinary anatomy. When serving on the National Council of Women in Kenya, she introduced her tree-planting idea and went on to develop it into the GBM. She estimates that her movement has planted 30 million trees. The Kenyan GBM has been a model for other African countries. She is internationally regarded as an eco-hero. She tells her story in *Unbowed: A Memoir* (2006).

Maathai is the first president of the African Union's ECOSOCC. The Kenyan National Council of Women and the GBM are two important civil society organizations in Africa.

---

* GBM Kenya, "Environmental Conservation/Tree Planting." Available online at *http://www.gbmna.org/w.php?id=13*.

** Quoted in Eco-Justice Ministries, "Eco-Justice Notes," October 15, 2004. Available online at *http://www.eco-justice.org/E041015.asp*.

(continued from page 84)

FOCUS ON WOMEN

Gender equality—basic equality between women and men—is a major goal of the AU, as enshrined in its Constitutive Act. In 2004, the Assembly of Heads of State and Government made a Solemn Declaration of Gender Equality in Africa. The ultimate responsibility for gender awareness and equality rests with the AU Commission and especially a special group within it called the Women, Gender and Development Directorate. The Directorate states:

> To date the women of Africa, like women elsewhere, have not been included as full, equal, and effective

stakeholders in processes that determine their lives. For example, women continue to have less access to education than men; they continue to have less employment and advancement opportunities; their role and contribution to national and continental development processes are neither recognized nor rewarded; they continue to be absent from decision-making; and, although they bear the brunt of conflicts, women are generally not included in peace negotiations or other initiatives in this regard.[29]

This comment echoes what many others have discovered. Although women are often the mainstays of families, the backbone of rural economies in sub-Saharan Africa, and the center of many civil society organizations, many lack access to land, formal employment, education, protection from family and civil violence, and reproductive and other forms of health care. Policymakers rarely think about women's needs and their important roles in developing African economies and society, but many groups have argued that it is imperative that they listen to and work with women.

The AU gives primary responsibility for including women's perspectives and needs in policy making to the commission, as well as guaranteeing a certain number of seats in the ECOSOCC to women. Recognizing that women are starting with many disadvantages, the AU intends to create certain areas of work that directly build women's empowerment, for example, encouraging special programs for women in science and technology. The Women, Gender and Development Directorate also ensures that the commission take gender equality into account in all its work, not just in special programs for women. When the AU is working on water problems, it is expected to consider the needs of women farmers and heads of household, and when it is working on resolving civil conflict, it must pay attention to the specific ways that women suffer from such violence, for example.

Female leaders like South Africa's deputy president Phumzile Mlambo-Ngcuka have fought for their right to be involved with the political affairs concerning their own countries and the AU. In order to minimize gender inequalities in Africa, the Women, Gender, and Development Directorate within the AU requires the consideration of female perspectives on all matters concerning the continent.

In August 2007, the AU held a special three-day conference on Women in Science and Technology, which brought together leading female scientists to discuss their role in science, technology, and African development. Botlhale Pema, from the South African Department of Science and Technology, explained:

> Last January, we had a summit of heads of state and government and they had the theme of science and technology for Africa's development, and one of the decisions that was taken was that we need to grow the constituency for science and technology to have more women and youth participating. . . . And this conference is a follow-up. We have now called on, under the umbrella of the African Union, all African women representatives and scientists from different member states to come and discuss this matter. . . . The African Union is determined to see to Africa's development, and they look at all aspects of development and women happen to be an important element in the development of Africa.[30]

One objective of the conference was to get some better statistics on how many women were participating in these fields; the estimate in South Africa is that women comprise about 36 percent of science and technology workers. A second objective was to identify what seem to be obstacles to women working in scientific fields. A third was to find solutions, including providing role models and supporting national groups of women in science in the African nations to which the AU could offer support.

HEALTH CARE IN AFRICA

Geography, history, and economics have contributed to the continent's exceptionally high vulnerability to and enormous burden of disease. A high proportion of mothers die in childbirth and of newborns die within their first year of life. Infection with HIV, the virus that destroys the human immune system and eventually leads to death, is widespread. Africans also suffer from other infectious diseases such as tuberculosis and malaria, deal with the consequences of pollution and lack of sanitation, and are increasingly struggling with chronic diseases like diabetes and heart disease. They suffer from malnutrition and experience injuries and diseases related to violence. It is difficult for African countries, with their limited resources and complex societies, to mount adequate responses. Most public-health experts say that millions of African deaths are needless, because although the diseases or conditions are preventable and/or treatable, the African states cannot make medical advances available to their populations. Often, African states partner with others—the World Health Organization (WHO), wealthy countries, international banks, nongovernmental organizations—to help deliver health care. African countries will be unable to develop economically and socially without substantial improvements in their peoples' health.

The AU Commission has fully endorsed the idea of the WHO that "African governments and their partners need to do more to build and reinforce health systems to deliver essential health care interventions to people living on this continent."[31] Its Council of Health Ministers has tried to coordinate national action and has produced an Africa Health Strategy for 2007–2015. The strategy focuses on building more effective health-care systems, increasing efforts to improve health, and developing stronger communities to decrease the disease burden. NEPAD (the New Partnership for Africa's Development) is urging governments to raise the amount they spend on health to 15 percent of their entire budget. These funds could be available if wealthier countries would consider debt reduction or forgiveness, freeing up the money that would otherwise go to repayment of loans for health care. Africa's special bank,

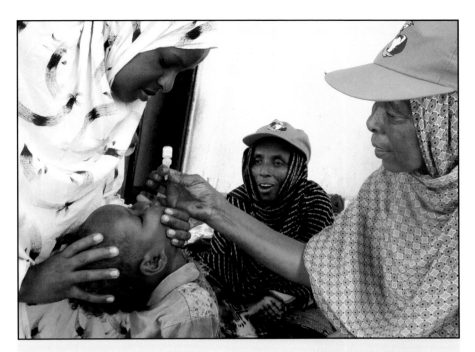

Due to their lack of economic development and large amounts of foreign debt, African countries are often unable to dedicate large amounts of their national budget to health care. The AU believes that spending 15 percent of a country's budget on health care could provide services to combat diseases and administer vaccines, as well as lower mother and infant mortality rates.

the African Development Bank, is also searching for ways of making money available to combat HIV/AIDS (the full-blown result of the virus), tuberculosis, and malaria.

The WHO and the AU met in 2004 to address the epidemic of disease and death among mothers and infants, seeking to reduce the high percentage of women who die during the delivery process and babies who die prematurely. Dr. Ebrahim Samba, the WHO regional director for Africa, informed the gathering of experts that the maternal mortality rate had risen since 1990 and that the death of African women in the child-bearing years is among the highest in the world. Infant mortality is even more dramatic. In Africa, 45 newborns die per 1,000 births as compared to 34 in Asia, 17 in Latin America, and just 5 in developed countries like the United States, the United Kingdom, France, and Germany.[32]

HIV/AIDS is the other terrible epidemic killing millions in Africa. Sub-Saharan Africa has 11 percent of the world's population but 60 percent of its AIDS (the full-blown disease) cases. In 2005, 25.8 million people in sub-Saharan Africa were living with AIDS, 3.2 million became newly infected, and 2.4 million died. In 16 countries, one out of 10 people is infected. More than half of the adults with AIDS in Africa are women; three-quarters of children with the disease are girls.[33]

HIV/AIDS has also increased the number of orphaned children in Africa; many parents die of it or of related diseases or become too incapacitated to care for them. Many children grow up in orphanages; some are adopted by relatives, others by foreigners and strangers. In many areas, such as the poor black townships of South Africa, school principals say that many of their pupils live in child-headed households. With no parent at home, usually because of AIDS deaths, the older children are helping younger ones survive.

Since the year 2000, AU leaders have been trying to make HIV/AIDS a top priority and to find a way for all Africans suffering from AIDS to get medical services, at the same time stepping up prevention and education efforts. In some countries, the efforts against this disease were lagging, often because their leaders were embarrassed to talk about AIDS, a disease transmitted sexually or by contaminated blood, generally in needles reused by some hospitals and used by addicts. And in South Africa there seemed to be a special problem within the political leadership.

Thabo Mbeki, while president of South Africa, had for many years been saying that AIDS was caused not by a virus, but by poverty. His view was contrary to that of nearly all scientists and public health officials around the world. Many people hold him largely responsible for South Africa's slow response to the epidemic and partly responsible for South Africa's high rate of HIV infection. His health minister recommended that people with AIDS eat beetroot and garlic as a cure for AIDS, and Mbeki fired the deputy health minister who was trying to develop a strong and scientifically based campaign against AIDS. Unlike South Africa, Uganda had a strong campaign and has cut the prevalence of the disease. Many HIV/AIDS activists have seen the AU as one force for bringing pressure on Mbeki and others who are lagging in leadership against the disease.

After facing pressure from African governments and international organizations, some Western drug companies have agreed to make life-prolonging AIDS drugs available at lower cost. Other international organizations and countries are also providing funding and expertise for fighting the epidemic.

Malaria, which kills about 200 children in Africa every day, is another major health challenge for most African countries. The disease is caused by the bite of female mosquitoes that carry the parasitic red blood cells from one person to another. Malaria is more widespread than HIV/AIDS, and it weakens the ability of an infected person to perform his or her daily functions. Although malaria can be controlled through medication and plenty of fluids, it can also cause prolonged periods of illness and death. Africans who live in areas where malaria-infested mosquitoes breed often use quinine as a preventative medicine against the disease. A genetic side effect of malaria is sickle cell anemia, which affects Africans and people of African descent in the Americas. Sickle cell anemia is a very painful and life-threatening disease which, ironically, protects against malaria by causing a mutation of the red blood cells. Adults with sickle cell anemia can become weakened by the disease when the mutated cells become stuck or cluster together in the bloodstream; children with the disease sometimes die prematurely as well.

PRESERVING AFRICAN CULTURE

The AU views the preservation of African cultural heritage as a vital part of its own revitalization. It sees the distinct African heritage as a source not only of meaning and pride for Africans, but also of business enterprise and economic development. Thabo Mbeki sees the culture as part of an African renaissance, or rebirth. This cultural heritage includes, among other things, the great historical monuments and sites of human history, living traditions of performing, the making of beautiful everyday objects, and the rich diversity of African languages.

Many of the official United Nations Economic, Social and Cultural Organization (UNESCO) World Heritage sites are in Africa. These are places of immense natural or cultural importance in the story of a common human heritage. They have been chosen after a long process of consideration. In South Africa alone there are eight such special places, ranging from the Cradle of Humankind area to Robben Island, where Nelson Mandela and other anti-apartheid activists were imprisoned. Robben Island, 6.8 miles (11 kilometers) offshore from Capetown, South Africa, is now somber testimony both to the cruelty of the apartheid system and to the triumph of the human spirit and the possibilities of democracy and peace. Ferries regularly take tourists to the island, and there are long waiting lines in most seasons of the year. The Cradle of Humankind area has one of the richest concentrations of hominid fossils, evidence of human evolution over the past 3.5 million years. The University of Witwatersrand in Johannesburg, South Africa, has helped research the area and has created a museum about the origins of humankind and early humans in the South Africa area.

Language traditions are sometimes referred to as Africa's intangible culture and an umbilical cord between Africa's past, present, and future generations. There are about 2,000 different languages used in Africa, a sign of the continent's long and complex history. Many of these languages are in danger of extinction, but programs like UNESCO's World Heritage Program are

A guide shows *(left to right)* South African deputy president Jacob Zuma, United Nations Secretary-General Kofi Annan, British anthropologist Jane Goodall, Kofi Annan's wife Nane, South African President Thabo Mbeki and First Lady Zanele Mbeki fossils on a visit to the Sterkfontein Caves in September 2002. These caves, which are a Cradle of Humankind World Heritage Site, hold some of the most significant fossils of our earliest human ancestors, including the remains of "Littlefoot," an almost complete hominid skeleton believed to be about 3.3 million years old.

encouraging university students and scholars to use technology to document this vast linguistic resource for Africa and for the world. Language preservation and usage are also central to the AU, and its development agenda. The AU declared 2006 as the Year of African Languages, and it encourages education in indigenous languages in both schools and community settings. All languages spoken in Africa have been declared official languages of the Union, but the AU uses English, French, Arabic, and Portuguese as its basic working languages; Swahili is also sometimes treated as a working language. On the top of most documents, *African Union* is written in English, Arabic, French, and Portuguese. Because of the existence of multiple languages in most African countries, most member states of the AU have policies of multi-lingualism—that is, policies that recognize more than one language, try to conduct public business in more than one language, and encourage learning and preservation of each country's languages.

The Future
of the AU

THE JOURNEY FROM THE ORGANIZATION OF AFRICAN UNITY to the African Union took four decades. As a twenty-first century organization, the AU hopes for a renaissance that includes improvement in the wealth, health, education, prosperity, and democracy across its member states and closer cooperation among all the countries on the African continent. The AU also aims for a strengthened role for Africa in the world. Its organizing body, the African Union Commission, has an enormous task ahead of it because it must find ways to achieve both African and global goals. The commission must interact with African populations and organizations and work with global and other region-wide organizations. A complicated history and differences among the member states make this work difficult but not impossible.

SUCCESS OF THE AU

The continent-wide organization in Africa has clearly moved with history, changing its objective from an end to colonialism under the OAU to African development and progress under the AU. It has redesigned its institutions so that the organization is not just a lot of important people talking to each other but also includes representatives of the people, in the Parliament and the ECOSOCC. The AU also has added some machinery with responsibility for human rights and peace and security. It is pursuing new economic strategies, and some of its regional economic communities seem to be moving forward. It is focusing upon health, education, and the environment. Many of its international partnerships—on the environment and on AIDS, for example—are constructive and creative initiatives.

CHALLENGES AHEAD

Economic challenges remain. Economic integration will be challenging for the less-wealthy member states, those with scant natural resources. Economic concerns will affect the ability of the AU to support the work of its various agencies and especially that of the ECOSOCC. Infrastructural needs will test the resources and political will of both African and international partnerships, while the AU Commission will face a daunting task in renegotiating political and trade treaties in order to meet a broad spectrum of human needs. The development of education and training will require patience, good will, and ongoing planning. The pressures from weak and war-torn states will always pose a threat to the limited resources available to the AU.

Different interests, old rivalries, and lingering ties to former colonial powers may drive a wedge between the AU's member states, creating challenges for political unity. The AU must confront the internal problems of its member states without making bad situations worse. It must find ways to confront authoritarian rulers effectively without weakening or even destroying the organization. The willingness of the AU to intervene in the affairs of disruptive states will help conquer some of the obstacles on the road to success, and international support will be useful.

The AU must pull together the vision and resources of its own many organizations and engage with outside organizations to help it achieve its overall goals. The road that the AU has mapped out requires diplomacy of the highest order, as well as the support of international organizations.

CHRONOLOGY

1884–85	Berlin Conference divides Africa among the European colonial powers at the height of the Scramble for Africa.
1950s	Libya and Ghana win independence.
1960s	Decolonization of much of Africa: Algeria, Mauritania, Mali, Niger, Senegal, the Gambia, Sierra Leone, Ivory Coast, Togo, Benin, Nigeria, Cameroon, Gabon, Congo, Botswana, Malawi, Zambia, Congo (Zaire), Uganda, Kenya, Somalia, Rwanda, Burundi, Chad, Burkina Faso, Madagascar, Lesotho, and Swaziland win their independence; Rhodesia unilaterally declares independence (UDI) from Britain.
1963	The Organization of African Unity (OAU) is formed.
1970s	Decolonization continues: Guinea Bissau, Mozambique, Angola win independence.
1975	West African states sign the Economic Community of West African States (ECOWAS) Treaty.
1980	Zimbabwe, formerly Rhodesia, becomes independent under the leadership of Robert Mugabe.
1991	OAU establishes the African Economic Community.
1994	Apartheid ends; South Africa has its first nonracial democratic election.
1999	Sirte Declaration announces intention to establish the African Union (AU).
2000	Lome Summit adopts the Constitutive Act of the African Union.
2001	The New Partnership for Africa's Development (NEPAD) is launched.
2002	Durban Summit officially launches the AU.

2004   Wangari Maathai wins the Nobel Peace Prize; the Economic, Social and Cultural Council (ECOSOCC) of the AU and the Pan-African Parliament are officially inaugurated.

2006   AU and UN Commission for Africa hold special summit on HIV/AIDS, tuberculosis, malaria.

2007   General Agwai of Nigeria leads AU forces in joint peacekeeping mission with United Nations forces in Darfur.

NOTES

Introduction

1. "Sanctions Against Rhodesia." *Time*, December 23, 1966. Available online at *http://www.time.com/time/magazine/article/0,9171,840760,00.htm*.

Chapter 1

2. "The Atlantic Charter" (1941). Available online at *http://usinfo.state.gov/usa/infousa/facts/democracy/53.htm*.
3. The World Bank Group. "Sub-Saharan Africa Data Profile." Available online at *http://devdata.worldbank.org*.

Chapter 2

4. Kwamina Panford, "Transition from the Organization of African Unity to the African Union," *Africa's Development in the Twenty-first Century*, Kwado Konadu-Agyemang and Kwamina Panford, eds. (Burlington, Vt.: Ashgate, 2006), 69–87.
5. United Nations General Assembly. "Declaration on the Granting of Independence to Colonial Countries and Peoples," Resolution 1514 of December 14, 1960. Available online at *http//www.ohchr.org*.
6. African Union. "The Constitutive Act." Available online at *http://www.africa-union.org*.
7. "Africa Hopes for New Beginning," BBC News, July 9, 2002. Available online at *http://news.bbc.co.uk/2/hi/africa/2116962.stm*.

Chapter 3

8. "Africa Union Summit—Briefing Note," Vol. 7, No. 1, January 28, 2007. Available online at *http://www.iisd.ca/africa*.

9. "Wade Criticizes Gradual Approach to Set Up AU Government," *Interests and Positions*, July 3, 2007. Available online at *http://www.apanews.net*.

10. "Qaddafi Calls for African Army of Two Million Soldiers," *Mail and Guardian*, June 28, 2007. Available online at *http://ww.mg.co.za*.

11. "Summit Debates Future of Africa," BBC News, July 3, 2007. Available online at *http://news.bbc.co.uk/2/hi/africa/6260274.stm*.

12. "Summit Focuses on African Unity," BBC News, July 1, 2007. Available online at *http://news.bbc.co.uk/2/hi/africa/6258072.stm*; "Ninth African Union Summit." Available online at *http://www.africanunion/root/au/Conferences/2007/june/summit/9thAUSummit.htm*.

Chapter 4

13. Lydia Polgreen, "Ruling Dynasty Seems to Start, Leaving Many Resentful," *New York Times*, February 9, 2005. Available online at *http://www.nytimes.com/2005/02/09/international/africa/09togo.html*; "AU Condemns Military Coup, Suspends Togo." Press release by African Union Peace and Security Council, February 25, 2005. Available online at *http://www.africafocus.org/docs05/togo0502.php*.

14. Polgreen, "West Africa Wins Again, With Twist," *New York Times*, February 27, 2005. Available online at *http://www.nytimes.com/2005/02/27/international/africa/27togo.html*.

15. United Nations Office for Coordination of Humanitarian Affairs. "Togo: Observers Sanction Elections While Opposition Cries Foul," October 18, 2007. Available online at *http://www.reliefweb.int*.

16.   Joseph Danladi Elvis Bot, "The AU and the Crisis in Darfur: Challenge of Regional Peacekeeping," *American Chronicle*, November 4, 2007. Available online at *http://www.american chronicle.com*; Alex de Waal, "The Wars of Sudan," *The Nation*, March 19, 2007. Available online at *http://www.thenation.com/doc/20070319/de_waal*; Jeffrey Gettleman, "Peacekeepers Without a Peace to Keep," *New York Times*, October 14, 2007. Available online at *http://www.nytimes.com/2007/10/14/weekinreview/14gettleman.html*; Gettleman, "Darfur Rebels Kill 10 in Peace Force," *New York Times*, October 1, 2007. Available online at *http://www.nytimes.com/2007/10/01/world/africa/01darfur.html*.

17.   Jeffry Gettleman, "Sudan Declares Cease-Fire at Darfur Peace Talks," *New York Times*, October 28, 2007. Available online at *http://www.nytimes.com/2007/10/28/world/africa/28darfur.html*.

18.   "Nigeria Asks Taylor to Leave," *The Perspective*, March 16, 2006. Available online at *http://www.theperspective.org/forum/0314200601.html*.

Chapter 5

19.   Shaohua Chen and Martin Ravallion, "How Have the World's Poorest Fared Since the Early 1980s?" *World Bank Research Observer*, Vol. 19, 2, pp. 141-169, Fall 2004. 20. NEPAD Secretariat, "Declaration on Democracy, Political, Economic, and Corporate Governance." Available online at *http://uneca.org/aprm/documents/book2.pdf*.

20.   NEPAD Secretariat, "Declaration on Democracy, Political, Economic, and Corporate Governance." Available online at *http://uneca.org/aprm/documents/book2.pdf*.

21.   "A Look at Water Resources in Africa." Available online at *www.wateryear2003.org*; "Africa's Potential Water

Wars," BBC News, November 15, 1999. Available online at *http://news.bbc.co.uk/2/hi/africa/454926.stm.*

22. Shaun Benton, "South Africa: National Income Per Person Increases by 22%," October 30, 2007. Available online at *http://www.allafrica.com/stories/200710300888.html*; Efam Dovi, "Bringing Water to the Continent's Poor," *Africa Renewal*, Vol. 21, No. 3, October 2007. Available online at *http://www.un.org/ecosocdev/geninfo/afrec/vol21/No3/213-water.html.*

23. John Donnelly, "Oil in Africa," *Boston Globe*. Available online at *http://www.boston.com/news/specials/oil_in_africa/*; Esther Pan, "China, Africa, and Oil," January 26, 2007. Available online at *http://www.cfr.org/publication/9557/#1.*

24. John Ghazvinian, "The Resource Curse: Why Africa's Oil Riches Don't Trickle Down to Africans," October 31, 2007. Available online at *http://knowledge.Wharton.upenn.edu/article.cfm?articleid=1830.*

25. U.S. Department of Commerce, International Trade Administration, "U.S.-Africa Trade Profile." Available online at *http://www.agoa.gov/resources.*

26. "2007 AGOA Report Shows Growth in US-Africa Trade," May 18, 2007. Available online at *http://www.ustr.gov/Document_Library/Press_Releases/2007/May/2007_AGOA_Report_Shows_Growth_in_US_Africa_Trade.html.*

Chapter 6

27. "The Need for ECOSOCC Process to Work." Available online at *http://www.ecosocc.org/articles/ecosoccProcess.pdf.*

28. Ibid.

29. African Union, Women, Gender, and Development Directorate, "Description and overview." Available online at *http://www.africa-union.org*

30. James Gutty, "African Union Holds Conference on Women in Science and Technology," August 30, 2007. Available online at *http://www.voanews.com.*

31. World Health Organization, *African Regional Health Report.* Available online at *http://www.afro.who.int/regional director/african_regional_health_report2006.pdf.*

32. World Health Organization, Africa, "WHO, African Union to Tackle High Rates of Maternal and Newborn Mortality," March 17, 2004. Available online at *http://www. afro.who.int/country_offices_press/2004/pr20040317.html.*

33. African Union, Special Summit on HIV/AIDS, Tuberculosis, Malaria, May 2006, "Aide Memoire." Available online at *http://www.africa-union.org/root/au/conferences/ past/2006/may/summit/summit.htm.*

BIBLIOGRAPHY

"Africa Hopes for New Beginning," BBC News. 9 July 2002. Available online. URL: http://news.bbc.co.uk/2/hi/africa/2116962.stm.

African Union Peace and Security Council. "AU Condemns Military Coup, Suspends Togo." 25 February 2005. Available online. URL: http://www.africafocus.org/docs05/togo0502.php.

African Union. "The Constitutive Act." Available online. URL: http://www.africa-union.org.

———. Special Summit on HIV/AIDS, Tuberculosis, Malaria. "Aide Memoire." May 2006. Available online. URL: http://www.africa-union.org/root/au/conferences/past/2006/may/summit/summit.htm.

"African Union Summit—Briefing Note." 28 January 2007. Available online. URL: http://www.iisd.Ca/Africa/brief/briefing0701e.html.

African Union. *Women, Gender and Developmetn Directorate.* "Description and Overview. Available online. URL: http://www.africa-union.org.

"Africa's Potential Water Wars." BBC New. 15 November 1999. Available online. URL: http://news.bbc.co.uk/2/hi/africa/454926.stm.

"The Atlantic Charter" 1941. Available online.URL: http://usinfo.state.gov/usa/infousa/facts/democracy/53.htm.

Beah, Ishmael. *A Long Way Gone. Memoirs of a Boy Soldier.* New York: Farrar, Straus and Giroux, 2007.

Benton, Shaun. "South Africa: National Income Per Person Increases by 22%." 30 October 2007. Available online. URL: http://allafrica.com/stories/200710300888.html.

Bot, Joseph Danladi Elvis. "The AU and the Crisis in Darfur: Challenge of Regional Peacekeeping." *American Chronicle* 4

November 2007. Available online. URL: http://www.american chronicle.com.

"Burkina Faso: Cotton Producers Celebrate WTO Ruling Against U.S. Subsidies." Available online. URL: http://www.irnnews.org.

Chen, Shaohua and Martin Ravallion. "How Have the World's Poorest Fared Since the Early 1980s?" *World Bank Research Observer* Vol. 19. No. 2 (Fall 2004): 141–169.

Cilliers, Jakkie and Kathryn Sturman. "Challenges Facing the AU's Peace and Security Council." African Security Review. Vol. 13. No. 1. Available online. URL: http://www.iss.co.za/pubs/ASR/13No1/CCilliers.pdf.

deWaal, Alex. "The Wars of Sudan." *The Nation.* 19 March 2007. Available online. URL: http://www.thenation.com/doc/20070319/de_waal.

Donnelly, John. "Oil in Africa." *Boston Globe.* Available online. URL: http://www.boston.com/news/specialis/oil_in_africa/.

Dovi, Efam. "Bringing Water to the Continent's Poor." *Africa Renewal.* Vol. 21. No. 3 (October 2007). Available online. URL: http://www.un.org/ecosocdev/geninfo/afrec/vol21/No3/213-water.html.

Eco-Justice Ministries. "Eco-Justice Notes." 15 October 2004. Available online. URL: http://www.eco-justice.org/E-041015.asp.

Esedebe, P. Olisanwuche. *Pan-Africanism: The Idea and Movement, 1776–1991,* 2nd ed. Washington, D.C.: Howard University Press, 1994.

"Fields of Hope: African Farmers Tell Their Stories." Available online. URL: http://www.oxfam.america.org/whatwedo/campaigns/agriculture/news_publications/fields_of_hope/index.html.

GBM Kenya. "Environmental Conservation/Tree Planting." Available online. URL: http://www.gbmna.org/w.php?id=13.

Gettleman, Jeffrey. "Darfur Rebels Kill 10 in Peace Force." *New York Times*, 1 October 2007. Available online. URL: http://www.nytimes.com/2007/10/01/world/africa/01darfur.html.

———. "Peacekeepers without a Peace to Keep." *New York Times*, 14 October 2007. Available online. URL: http://www.nytimes.com/2007/10/14/weekinreview/14gettleman.html.

———. "Sudan Declares Cease-Fire at Darfur Peace Talks." *New York Times*. 28 October 2007. Available online. URL: http://www.nytimes.com/2007/10/28/world/africa/28darfur.html.

Ghazvinian, John. "The Resource Curse: Why Africa's Oil Riches Don't Trickle Down to Africans." 31 October 2007. Available online. URL: http://knowledge.wharton.upenn.edu/article.cfm?articleid=1830.

Gordon, April and Donald Gordon, Eds. *Understanding Contemporary Africa*, 3rd ed. Boulder, Colo.: Lynne Rienner, 2001.

Gutty, James. "African Union Holds Conference on Women in Science and Technology." 30 August 2007. Available online. URL: http://www.voanews.com.

"A Look at Water Resources in Africa." Available online. URL: http://www.wateryear2003.org.

Mboweni, T.T. "The Benefits of Being a Good Host: The FIFA World Cup and the South African Economy," 20 March 2007. Available online. URL: http://www.reservebank.co.za/internet/publication.nsf.

Mutume, Gumisai. "Mounting Opposition to Northern Farm Subsidies." *Africa Recovery*, Vol. 17 No. 1. (May 2003). Available online. URL: http://www.un.org/ecosocdev/geninfor/afrec/vol17no1/171agri4.htm.

"The Need for ECOSOCC Process to Work." Available online. URL: http://www.ecosocc.org/articles/ecosoccProcess.pdf.

NEPAD Secretariat. "Declaration on Democracy, Political, Economic and Corporate Governance." Available online. URL: http://uneca.org/aprm/documents/book2.pdf.

"Nigeria Asks Taylor to Leave," The Perspective. 16 March 2006. Available online. URL: http://www.theperspective.org/forum/0314200601.html.

"Ninth African Union Summit." Available online. URL: http://www.africanunion/root/au/Conferences/2007/june/summit/9thAUSummit.htm.

Nkrumah, Kwame. *I Speak of Freedom*, in Modern History Sourcebook. Available online. URL: http://www.fordham.edu/halsall/mod/1961nkrumah.html.

Packer, Corinne and Donald Rukare. "The New African Union and Its Constitutive Act." *American Journal of International Law*. Vol 96. No. 2 (April 2002), 365–379.

Pan, Esther. "China, Africa, and Oil." 26 January 2007. Available online.URL: http://www.cfr.org/publication/9557/#1.

Panford, Kamina. "Transition from the Organization of African Unity to the African Union." *African Development in the Twenty-first Century*. eds. Kwado Konadu-Agyemang and Kwamina Panford, Burlington, VT: Ashgate, 2006.

Polgreen, Lydia. "Ruling Dynasty Seems to Start, Leaving Many Resentful." *New York Times*, 9 February 2005. Available online. URL: http://www.nytimes.com/2005/02/09/international/africa/09togo.html.

———. "West Africa Wins Again, With Twist." *New York Times*, 27 February 2005. Available online. URL: http://www.nytimes.com/2005/02/27/international/africa/27togo.html.

"Qaddafi Calls for African Army of Two Million Soldiers." *Mail and Guardian*, 28 June 2007. Available online. URL: http://www.mg.co.za.

Rice, Xan. "Ready or Not." *Observer*, 3 (June 2007). Available online. URL: http://football.guardian.co.uk/print/0,,329948830-103,00.html.

"Sanctions Against Rhodesia." *Time*, 23 December 1966. Available online. URL: http://www.time.com/time/magazine/article/0,9171,840760,00.htm.

"Summit Debates Future of Africa." BBC News. 3 July 2007. Available online. URL: http://news.bbc.co.uk/2/hi/africa/6260274.stm.

"Summit Focuses on African Unity." BBC News. 1 July 2007. Available online. URL: http://news.bbc.co.uk/2/hi/africa/6258072.stm.

United Nations General Assembly. "Declaration on the Granting of Independence to Colonial Countries and Peoples," 14 December 1960. Available online. URL: http://www.ohchr.org.

United Nations Office for Coordination of Humanitarian Affairs. "Togo: Observers Sanction Elections While Opposition Cries Foul." 18 October 2007. Available online. URL: http://www.reliefweb.int.

United States Department of Commerce International Trade Administration. "U.S.-Africa Trade Profile." Available online. URL: http://www.agoa.gov/resources.

"Wade Criticizes Gradual Approach to Set UP AU Government." *Interests and Positions*. 3 July 2007. Available online. URL: http://www.apanews.net.

The World Bank Group. "Sub-Saharan Africa Data Profile." Available online. URL: http://devdata.worldbank.org.

World Health Organization African Regional Health Report. Available online. URL: http://www.afro.who.int/regional director/african_regional_health_report2006.pdf.

World Health Organization, Africa. "WHO, African Union to Tackle High Rates of Maternal and Newborn Mortality." 17 March 2004. Available online.URL: http://www.afro.who.int/ country_offices_press/2004/pr20040317.html.

"2007 AGOA Report Shows Growth in US-Africa Trade." 18 May 2007. Available online. URL: http://www.ustr.gov/ Document_Library/Press_Releases/2007/May/2007_ AGOA_Report_Shows_Growth_in_US_Africa_Trade.html.

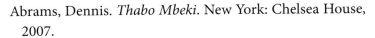

FURTHER READING

Abrams, Dennis. *Thabo Mbeki*. New York: Chelsea House, 2007.

Beah, Ishmael. *A Long Way Gone: Memoirs of a Boy Soldier*. New York: Farrar, Straus and Giroux, 2007.

Bul Dau, John with Michael S. Sweeny. *God Grew Tired of Us: A Memoir*. Washington, D.C.: National Geographic, 2007.

Coltrell, Robert. *South Africa: A State of Apartheid*. New York: Chelsea House, 2005.

Domingo, Vernon. *South Africa*. New York: Chelsea House, 2003.

French, Howard. *A Continent for the Taking: The Tragedy and Hope of Africa*. New York: Vintage, 2005.

Goodman, David. *Fault Lines: Journeys into the New South Africa*. Berkeley: University of California Press, 1999.

Koestler-Grack, Rachel. *Kofi Annan*. New York: Chelsea House, 2007.

Maathai, Wangari. *Unbowed: A Memoir*. New York: Knopf, 2006.

Oppong, Joseph R. and Esther Oppong. *Ghana*. New York: Chelsea House, 2003.

Rusesabagina, Paul. *An Ordinary Man: An Autobiography*. New York: Penguin, 2007.

WEB SITES

Africa Action
http://www.africaaction.org

African Cultural Center USA
http://www.africanculturalcenter.org

African Medical and Research Foundation
http://www.amref.org

The African Union
http://www.africa-union.org/root/au/index/index.htm

British Broadcasting Corporation's Africa News
http://news.bbc.co.uk/2/hi/africa/default.stm

Michigan State University High
School Curriculum on Africa
http://exploringafrica.matrix.msu.edu/students/curriculum/

Oxfam Committee for Famine Relief
(OXFAM)-West Africa Program
http://www.oxfam.org/en/programs/development/wafrica/

Oxfam Committee for Famine Relief
(OXFAM)-Horn of Africa Program
http://www.oxfam.org/en/programs/development/hafrica/

World Health Organization
http://whqlibdoc.who.int/afro/2006/9290231033_rev_eng.pdf

FILMS

Camp de Thiaroye and *Moolade* (Directed by Ousmane
Sembene)

Cry Freedom (Directed By Richard Attenborough)

Hotel Rwanda (Directed by Terry George)

La Vie Est Belle (Directed by Benoit Lamy and Mweza
Ngangura)

Sometimes in April (Directed by Raoul Peck)

The Last King of Scotland (Directed by Kevin Macdonald)

The Little Girl Who Stole the Sun (Directed by Djibril Mambety)

The Silences of the Palace (Directed by Moufida Tlatli)

Tilai (Directed by Idrissa Ouedraogo)

Tsotsi (Directed by Gavin Hood)

PICTURE CREDITS

PAGE

INDEX

ABOUT THE CONTRIBUTORS

DIEDRE L. BADEJO is professor of African and African Diaspora Studies and Dean of the College of Letters, Arts, and Social Sciences at California State University at East Bay. She is former associate dean of curriculum and chair of Pan-African Studies at Kent State University. She lived in Nigeria and Ghana for many years and is the author of several chapters and articles on African topics. She has a doctorate in Comparative Literature with an African history concentration, a Master's in African Area Studies from UCLA, and B.A. in English from the University of Southern California.

PEGGY KAHN is professor of political science at the University of Michigan-Flint. She teaches world and European politics. She has been a social studies volunteer in the Ann Arbor, Michigan, public schools and helps prepare college students to become social studies teachers. She has a Ph.D. in political science from the University of California, Berkeley and a B.A. in history and government from Oberlin College.